Freedom of the Press
and Fair Trial

Freedom of the Press and Fair Trial

FINAL REPORT WITH RECOMMENDATIONS

by THE SPECIAL COMMITTEE ON RADIO,
TELEVISION, AND THE ADMINISTRATION
OF JUSTICE OF THE ASSOCIATION OF
THE BAR OF THE CITY OF NEW YORK

Judge Harold R. Medina, Chairman

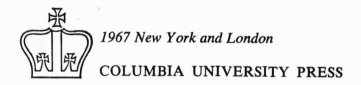

1967 New York and London
COLUMBIA UNIVERSITY PRESS

Final Report with Recommendations
by
the Special Committee on Radio, Television, and
the Administration of Justice
of The Association of the Bar
of the City of New York

FREDERICK vP. BRYAN   MacNEIL MITCHELL

E. THAYER DRAKE   MICHAEL J. MURPHY

FRANK S. HOGAN   WHITNEY NORTH SEYMOUR

DAVID M. LEVITAN   SAMUEL J. SILVERMAN

HARRIS B. STEINBERG

HAROLD R. MEDINA
Chairman

ROBERT D. WACHS   GENE McHAM
Research Assistant   *Secretary*

INTRODUCTION

IN the Fall of 1965 this Special Committee of The Association of the Bar of the City of New York issued its Interim Report, entitled *Radio, Television, and the Administration of Justice: A Documented Survey of Materials,* published by Columbia University Press. The *Documented Survey of Materials* was intended for use in all parts of the United States as a sort of law school volume of Cases and Materials. The data collected were arranged in such a way as to present for discussion and further study numerous examples of major and minor problems in the Free Press and Fair Trial controversy, in the hope that such materials would be useful to those interested in finding some reasonable and practical answers to many, if not most, of the problems. At that time we refrained from any interpretation of this factual material and said that, after further study, we would report our conclusions and recommendations. Such is the purpose of this Final Report.

As we are now of the opinion that the First Amendment guarantee of free speech and free press and the critical importance of the concept of freedom of communication that underlies this guarantee preclude, on both constitutional and policy grounds, direct controls of the news media by a governmental scheme of legislative or judicial regulation, the general theme of this Final Report is to evaluate and state the steps that we think should be taken by the judicial establishment, understood as including the courts and the judges, the Bar and the law enforcement agencies, state and federal, to put its own house in order.

We think our *Documented Survey of Materials* demonstrates the need of prompt remedial action. Accordingly, we have grouped our comments and recommendations under the following headings: "The First Amendment"; "The Lawyers and Recommended New Canon 20"; "Police and Other Law Enforcement Agencies and Recommended Code of Regulations"; "The Courts and the Judges"; "Recent Developments"; and we have included as an Appendix the Opinion of Justice Clark in Sheppard v. Maxwell, 384 U.S. 333 (1966).

Much may be done and much is being done to foster colloquia between representatives of the news media and the judges and lawyers. The two-volume publication of the Joint Hearings of the Subcommittee on Constitutional Rights and the Subcommittee on Improvements in Judicial Machinery of the United States Senate Judiciary Committee has provided a mass of useful information. We are grateful to Senators Sam J. Ervin, Jr., and Joseph D. Tydings for the broad scope of these hearings and the diversity of views expressed by interested persons. Naturally, the voluntary codes and joint statements of principles now in force are first steps. Cooperation between the news media and the judicial establishment, as we have above defined it, will not only lead to the elimination of misunderstandings and the mutual recriminations that have impaired progress in the past; it will also lead to restraint and the further development of controlling principles. As the Advisory Committee on Fair Trial and Free Press, of which Judge Paul C. Reardon is Chairman, as part of the American Bar Association Project on Minimum Standards for Criminal Justice, has undertaken the management of some of these colloquia, we have felt that we should confine our efforts to other aspects of the general problem. Nor do we discuss the use of radio and television in courtrooms in view of the all but universal elimination of these media in federal and state courts as disclosed in Chapter IV of our Interim Report, entitled "Canons of Ethics, Court Rules, Opinions of Courts, and Analogous Rulings Affecting the Use of Radio and Television In and Around the Courts."

Following the policy reflected in our Interim Report, our continuing effort is to view the Free Press and Fair Trial issues as national rather than local in scope. But we have not attempted to make our documentation exhaustive and complete. On the contrary, our endeavor has been to present typical groupings of incidents, whether manifested in newspapers, over the radio, or on television, with an eye to constitutional questions arising under the First, Fifth, Sixth, and Fourteenth Amendments and a variety of allied policy questions affecting the community interest in the prompt, impartial, and just disposition of civil and criminal cases.

It is not the purpose or intent of this Final Report to charge any particular group with responsibility for the present unsatisfactory state of affairs. Long-continued practices and abuses in the matter of publicity connected with both civil and criminal judicial proceedings and the participants therein have grown and burgeoned, aided by modern improvements in the art of communications. The bench and the Bar, the law enforcement agencies, the news media, and the community at large have each made their respective contribution. What we do suggest is action that we hope may result in appropriate controls of the lawyers and the law enforcement officials, under the auspices of the lawyers and the police themselves, more positive and effective action by the courts and the judges, and a larger measure of self-restraint by the news media.

We do not pretend to be the source of all wisdom in this or any other field of investigation. The dialogue that has progressed without abatement since the aftermath of the assassination of President John F. Kennedy, and for a long time prior thereto, will no doubt continue, and this is as it should be. Since our investigation started in 1963 there has been some improvement, and a significant step forward was made by the statement of policy issued by the Toledo *Blade* and the Toledo *Times* on August 21, 1966, acting in cooperation with the local Toledo Bar Association. But there is steady progress in the right direction, with occasional setbacks, as appears in Chapter V of this Final Report, "Recent Developments." We can only hope that the contents of this Final Report will be of some assistance to those both within and outside the judicial establishment who will in the end decide what is to be done further to remedy the present intolerable state of affairs.

This Special Committee was organized in 1963 by Herbert Brownell, then President of The Association of the Bar of the City of New York. In the following year during the administration of Samuel I. Rosenman as President of the Association under the same Chairman, the personnel of the Committee was changed and the objectives of the Committee clarified. And this Final Report was completed in the administration of Russell D. Niles. To each of these Presidents of the Association the Committee is grateful for unstinted cooperation and assistance. We are glad again to express our gratitude to the Ford Foundation for its generous grant of $25,000 to defray the expenses incident to our investigation and the preparation and publication of our Interim and Final Reports.

We have received assistance and cooperation from many sources. H. Richard Uviller, Assistant District Attorney of New York County in charge of Appeals Bureau, and John G. Bonomi, Chief Counsel of the Committee on Grievances of The Association of the Bar of the City of New York, were most helpful in connection with the preparation of Chapter II of this Final Report, "The Lawyers and Recommended New Canon 20." The Committee was especially fortunate in having had the assistance and close collaboration of Leonard E. Reisman, President of the College of Police Science of the City University of New York, in connection with Chapter III and the formulation of our Recommended Code of Regulations for Police and Other Law Enforcement Agencies.

Murray J. Laulicht, Burton Lehman, and Glenn E. Coven, Jr.,

before, during, and after their incumbencies as my Law Clerks, supplemented the work of our Research Assistant, Robert D. Wachs.

HAROLD R. MEDINA
Chairman

United States Courthouse
New York City
September, 1966

Contents

I

THE FIRST AMENDMENT

OUR documented survey of materials on radio, television, and the administration of justice, brings into sharp focus the many impacts news media have on investigatory and judicial proceedings. The deleterious effects on such proceedings of unrestrained reporting and commentary by newspapers, radio, and television are too widespread and too well documented to be gainsaid. After exhaustive study, however, we have concluded that direct controls on the radio and television industries and on the press by a governmental scheme of regulation are untenable in the light of the First Amendment's guarantee of free speech and free press.

The First Amendment's mandate that "Congress shall make no law . . . abridging the freedom of speech, or of the press" has a cherished place in our society. Through the due process clause of the Fourteenth Amendment, it is also applied to the states, most of which have similar constitutional or legislative provisions, and it is the major obstacle to any attempt legislatively or judicially to curb the excesses of the news media in this country. Moreover, the courts and the Bar, no less than the press, jealously protect First Amendment freedoms and look with a jaundiced eye on attempts to circumscribe the free flow of information.

CONTEMPT OF COURT

It is frequently suggested that, through the exercise of the contempt power, which courts possess either inherently or by virtue of enabling legislation, the courts have the power to curtail excesses of the news media as they affect judicial proceedings. And some commentators have asserted that a more vigorous use of this power to punish interferences with the administration of justice will result in deterring harmful publications. After diligent examination of these suggestions, however, the Committee is unpersuaded, as to either their wisdom or validity.

History of the Contempt Power

The statute governing the summary contempt power of a federal court, 18 U.S.C., Section 401, gives it power to punish summarily "misbehavior" occurring "in its presence or so near thereto as to obstruct the administration of justice." This legislation has been on the books in much the same form since 1831, Act of March 2, 1831, 44 Stat. 487, but through a process of judicial construction has been so limited as to be inapplicable to out-of-court statements. Toledo Newspaper Co. v United States, 247 U.S. 402 (1918), construed the words "presence" and "near" in the summary contempt statute as going to the question whether an out-of-court statement *caused* an obstruction to the administration of justice. Under this interpretation such an extrajudicial publication could be punished summarily as a contempt of court. But, in 1941, *Toledo Newspaper* was overruled, and the Supreme Court read the words "presence" and "near" to import geographical rather than causative considerations. Nye v. United States, 313 U.S. 33, 47-53 (1941). By this construction of the statute, federal courts were, and to this day still are, bereft of statutory summary power to punish statements made outside their presence. By virtue of various enactments of state legislatures many state courts are also precluded from punishing contempts by publication summarily. See Annotation, 69 A.L.R.2d 676 (1960).

To be sure, there do exist remedies other than summary contempt proceedings through which a court might seek to punish publication of statements deemed disruptive of the administration of justice. In the federal as well as the state sphere, authorities may proceed by indictment and full criminal trial under laws relating to the obstruction and corruption of justice. And in some states, nonsummary procedures for contempt by publication may be used. However, in all these instances the problems of proving intent to obstruct justice or to affront the dignity of a court have made these remedies ineffective, except in the most outrageous and extreme circumstances.

In addition, the Committee has considered in its study of this subject various proposed statutes that would make it a crime, punishable by fine and imprisonment after normal procedures such as indictment and trial by jury, to publish certain types of information deemed likely to prejudice seriously a fair trial. Some of these proposed statutes list, more or less exhaustively, the specific items which may not be publicized; others are much broader, proscribing generally the publication of material which may be prejudicial to the right to a fair trial by an impartial jury. Interim Report, pp. 294-301.

The Committee is of the opinion that danger of erosion of the most important of all our freedoms is bound to inhere in this type of legislation, whether couched in simple and misleading generalities or in lengthy and detailed enumeration of the items of news within the area of prohibition.

Contempt by Publication

Summary contempt proceedings and prosecutions pursuant to the provisions of legislation which make it a criminal offense to publish matter interfering with a fair trial also pose serious constitutional problems. Supreme Court decisions make it unlikely, in the opinion of the Committee, that a conviction for contempt by publication or a similar criminal offense will be upheld. Although it has been discarded in many other free speech–free press situations, the "clear and present danger" test still has great vitality in this field and places an almost insurmountable burden of proof on the prosecuting authorities.

The leading case placing constitutional limits on the power to punish contempts by publication is Bridges v. California, 314 U.S. 252 (1941), which was also the decision for a companion case, *Times-Mirror Co. v. Superior Court.* In *Bridges,* a labor leader publicly criticized a state judge's decision in a labor case as "outrageous"; in *Times-Mirror,* a newspaper urged and publicly pressured a judge not to grant probation to two men convicted of assault. And in both cases, the judges sitting without juries held the utterers in contempt and were affirmed by the state's highest court. On review by the Supreme Court, Justice Black, for the majority, after noting the absence of a specific California legislative determination that out-of-court statements should be punished, applied the "clear and present danger" test as the measure against which the constitutionality of these impositions on free speech and free press were to be judged. The "minimum compulsion of the Bill of Rights" requires that "the substantive evil must be extremely serious and the degree of imminence extremely high before utterances can be punished." 314 U.S. at 263. The Court rejected the "reasonable tendency" test which previously had been the standard, while the dissenters, led by Justice Frankfurter, argued for retention of the "reasonable tendency" standard. Using "clear and present danger" as above defined as the yardstick, the Court reversed the convictions of Bridges and the Times-Mirror.

Following *Bridges* by a few years were Pennekamp v. Florida, 328 U.S. 331 (1946), and Craig v. Harney, 331 U.S. 367 (1947), each of which involved editorial criticisms of judges for the purpose of influencing their decisions in nonjury matters. The Supreme Court reversed summary convictions for contempt in both instances, holding fast to and strengthening the "clear and present danger" test. As recently as 1962, in Wood v. Georgia, 370 U.S. 375, the Court once again held that the evidence adduced was insufficient to show a "clear and present danger" to the administration of justice. In that case, a sheriff had issued press releases concerning a judge's action in convening a grand jury to investigate alleged bloc voting, and it had been established that the grand jury read the releases.

It must be kept in mind, of course, that none of these cases involved a petit jury in a criminal or civil trial, instances with which the Committee is most concerned. Indeed, the Court in each case was careful to warn that they were only deciding on the particular facts before them and were not setting down the outer limits on state power to protect the integrity of the administration of justice through contempt. In *Wood,* in fact, Chief Justice Warren noted that the Court "need not pause here to consider the variant factors that would be present in a case involving a petit jury. . . . And of course the limitations on free speech assume a different proportion when expression is directed toward a trial as compared to a grand jury investigation." 370 U.S. at 389–90. Whether this dictum foreshadows a broader range for the contempt power in regard to trials before petit juries is, however, far from clear. In Maryland v. Baltimore Radio Show, 338 U.S. 912 (1950), a radio station was held in contempt for broadcasting news of the confession and past criminal record of a man accused of the sensational murder of a young girl. The defense counsel had waived a jury trial because of the widespread hostility engendered by this publicity. The Maryland Court of Appeals, although fully cognizant of the fact that an impartial jury trial might have been impossible, reversed the contempt conviction on the ground that *Bridges, Pennekamp,* and *Craig* protected the broadcaster. The Supreme Court, however, denied certiorari, and Justice Frankfurter expressed his views in a separate opinion.

The Contempt Power Today

Thus it can be cogently argued that as the *Bridges, Pennekamp, Craig,* and *Wood* decisions stressed the fact that the publications were aimed at elected judges and also emphasized the supposedly thick-skinned nature of judges as reasons for allowing out-of-court criticism of them, these decisions do not foreclose the question of a court's power to restrain the press when a jury is involved. Nevertheless, the Committee is of the opinion that the guarantees of the First Amendment will prevent the use of the contempt power to control the news media even where the impartiality of a petit jury is endangered. Moreover, the Committee feels that the "clear and present danger" test would be applied as well to criminal prosecutions and nonsummary contempt proceedings, thereby making it unlikely that they would pass constitutional muster. Although the *Bridges-Wood* cases are not controlling precedents, they do manifest a highly protective attitude on the part of the Supreme Court toward the press. Our conclusion as to the probable course of adjudication under the First Amendment in contempt cases involving the types of newspaper stories and radio and television broadcasts set forth in our Interim Report (*Radio, Television, and the Administration of Justice: A Documented Survey of Materials*) is borne out by a careful analysis of the conflicting theories that lie behind the series of Supreme Court decisions above discussed.

On the one hand, there is the theory, reflected in Justice Frankfurter's dissent in *Bridges* and his opinion in connection with the denial of certiorari in *Baltimore Radio Show,* that "trial by newspaper" could result in fine or imprisonment for contempt of court if it was established by proof that the publication or broadcast had a reasonable tendency to interfere with a fair and impartial trial. That such inference exists is evident from the number of typical instances set forth in our Interim Report, showing utterances affecting witnesses as well as defendants, supposed confessions, prior convictions, statements of opinion on the subject of the guilt or innocence of those accused of crime, and a totally uninhibited series of similar publications or broadcasts on the part of the news media.

But the theory that prevailed was that a reasonable tendency to interfere with the administration of justice was not enough.

Instead, it was held that the "clear and present danger" test should govern. The substantive evil to be remedied was that of "unfair administration of justice," or "the possibility of causing unfair disposition of a pending case." Doubtless, decisions by judges or juries should be made "on the evidence and arguments properly advanced in open court," and "trials are not like elections, to be won through the use of the meeting hall, the radio, and the newspaper." Nevertheless, the Supreme Court held that the First Amendment must be given "the broadest scope that could be countenanced in an orderly society" or "the broadest scope that explicit language, read in the context of a liberty-loving society, will allow." On this basis it was determined that an adjudication of contempt, whether by a state or federal court, could be permitted to stand only if the "clear and present danger" to a fair trial was demonstrated to be "extremely serious and the degree of imminence extremely high."

Thus as late as 1962 the clear and present danger test was applied to a contempt by publication charge although that test has been abandoned in many other, if not all, fields relating to limitations on the freedoms of speech and of the press. It is our considered opinion that the common "garden-variety" newspaper accounts and broadcasts that have been in vogue for many years will not be found to measure up to this test. Nor, as will appear, is it likely that the Supreme Court as now constituted will, nor do we think it should, make the test less onerous. Furthermore, more recent decisions of the Supreme Court suggest that the Court has found in judicial housecleaning an alternative approach to controlling prejudicial publicity that is more consistent with the traditional American preference for an uncensored press. If this approach is successful, the need for direct controls over the press will be diminished and thus the chance that the Supreme Court will sustain their use will lessen. Certainly it is doubtful that the Court will endorse a less onerous test for the use of the contempt power against the news media until the courts and the judges, the lawyers and the law enforcement officials have made a more serious effort to clean house.

Estes and Sheppard

This alternative solution has been developed in the cases of Estes v. Texas, 381 U.S. 532 (1965) and Sheppard v. Maxwell, 384 U.S. 333 (1966). In *Estes,* the Court announced its conclusion that the full scope of free press must at times be limited by a sturdy application of the requirements of fair trial. Justice Clark wrote:

The free press has been a mighty catalyst in awakening public interest in governmental affairs, exposing corruption among public officers and employees and generally informing the citizenry of public events and occurrences, including court proceedings. While maximum freedom must be allowed the press in carrying on this important function in a democratic society its exercise must necessarily be subject to the maintenance of absolute fairness in the judicial process. [381 U.S. at 539.]

A majority of the Court held that the televising of a notorious criminal trial was inherently a denial of due process and thereby firmly established the proposition that a conviction obtained in a courtroom where the press were permitted to misbehave would be reversed. This decision was extended in *Sheppard* to trials poisoned by an environment of prejudicial publicity. The underlying rationale of that decision is that the massive and prejudicial publicity during Dr. Sheppard's trial for the alleged murder of his wife deprived him of his constitutional right to a fair trial and could have been avoided had the trial judge properly exercised his power "to control the publicity about the trial." It would seem that the Supreme Court has chosen to strengthen the constitutional standard for the conduct of a trial when the issue is whether a conviction obtained in an environment of prejudicial publicity can stand and thus to give the various state judges and prosecutors an incentive to reduce the flow of prejudicial information to the press.

In making clear the Court's position, Justice Clark set out in *Sheppard* a variety of actions which a trial judge would be expected to take should a given case become a *cause célèbre* and specific reference is made to the failure of the trial judge to "impose control over the statements made to the news media by counsel, witnesses, and especially the Coroner and police officers." The recommended steps are analyzed in detail in Chapter IV of this Final Report dealing with the courts and the judges.

Even though the standard for reversal has become less tolerant of publicity, the "clear and present danger" standard for contempt seems unchanged. Justice Clark's opinion reiterated the Court's strong reluctance to support proceedings directly aimed at the newspapers and the broadcasting companies. Citing *Craig v. Harney,* to which reference has already been made, the opinion states: "And where there was 'no threat or menace to the integrity of the trial,' we have consistently required that the press have a free hand, even though we sometimes deplored its sensationalism."

True it is that the opinion also states that the Justices "do not consider what sanctions might be available against a recalcitrant press," but in context this statement refers to action that might have been taken after the news media had deliberately frustrated or disobeyed the controls that were imposed by the trial judge. In any event, this remark also suggests that before direct controls on the press are permissible, the alternatives must be pursued.

Another relevant point of view is expressed in Ronald L. Goldfarb's *The Contempt Power* (1963) at page 193, as follows:

Acceptance of what is now a minority view, that First Amendment rights are absolutes, would clearly resolve all these issues. The wisdom as well as the popularity of such an attitude is open to debate, which it is not the function of this book to include or evaluate, except in so far as it affects the present subject. In the contempt context, it is not unreasonable to suggest a complete First Amendment protection of the press. Since judges may be left to private actions for defamatory criticism by the press and ought to be able to withstand nondefamatory criticism, the principal reason for the constructive contempt power is to protect the fairness of the trial itself. This can be accomplished in ways less calculated to interfere with vital constitutional rights like freedom of the press. In nonpress cases, a more restricted freedom has prevailed, though the power to affect trials is generally less than that of the press.

The British System

The British courts have the power to punish summarily as contempt any publication with respect to a pending or incipient criminal prosecution or civil suit that may tend to interfere with the course of justice. This power is exercised quite vigorously, and as a result comment on cases in Great Britain and the Commonwealth is almost nonexistent, save for accounts of events in open court. But to suggest that we adopt this system in the United States ignores the differences between our constitutional tradition of free expression and that of the British, as Justice Black's opinion in *Bridges,* 314 U.S. at 263-66, makes quite clear. Also there is an excellent discussion of these differences between the American and the British holdings in the concurring opinion of Vice Chief Justice Bernstein in *Phoenix Newspapers, Inc. v. Superior Court,* decided on October 5, 1966, by the Supreme Court of Arizona, sitting in banc. This case is further examined in Chapter IV, "The Courts and the Judges." In addition, it must be realized that the British power to punish for contempt is not restricted solely to instances when a publication may prejudice a fair trial; it is sometimes used to vindicate the outraged dignity of the court, and this too seems inconsistent with the American conception of freedom of speech and freedom of the press.

Summary

In sum, our conclusion is that constitutional guarantees would stand in the way of most efforts to regulate the relationship between trials and the media, whether by legislation or by use of the contempt power. And perhaps this is as it should be, for such efforts would embroil the courts in constant conflicts between the courts and the media, which would naturally resist official efforts to restrict their freedom. Such conflicts would not serve to improve the administration of justice but would only estrange those whose common interest should be improvement. This would result in many criminal cases, which are now adversary proceedings between the state and the defendant, also becoming adversary proceedings between the courts and the media, and we cannot believe that this would advance the public interest. Accordingly, because we believe that as a matter of both constitutional law and policy, an approach through legislation or extension of the contempt power is neither feasible nor wise, our recommendations proceed along other lines.

Before reaching them we think it proper to comment on the so-called "right of the people to know," often cited by the media not only as a reason for pursuing their news objectives but also as an excuse or justification for not doing anything effective to correct existing conditions.

"THE RIGHT OF THE PUBLIC TO KNOW"

The literature on the subject of Free Press and Fair Trial contains repeated references to "the right of the public to know." But the invocation of this phrase solves nothing, for there is also "the right of the accused to a fair trial." All concerned must frankly face the fact that neither of these "rights" is absolute, for they conflict and must be reconciled in a manner calculated to cause the least injury to either value.

The administration of justice, and of criminal justice in particular, touches the operation of American democracy at the quick. It is highly desirable and is an undoubted part of the constitutional mandate itself that the processes of law enforcement be open to the public view, both for the purpose of protecting the innocent and bringing the guilty to boot and for the purpose of exposing incompetence, venality, or corruption on the part of those who arrest and prosecute and those who may sit in the seats of judgment. But there is, of course, no overriding policy consideration that favors the disclosure of facts at a time that will hamper investigation or make it more difficult either to acquit the innocent or to convict the guilty. It must be remembered that "public trial" is in essence an institutional safeguard designed to ensure the achievement of the system's ultimate objective: a fair trial. As stated by Chief Justice Warren in his concurring opinion in *Estes*:

The guarantee of a public trial confers no special benefit on the press, the radio industry or the television industry. A public trial is a necessary component of an accused's right to a fair trial and the concept of public trial cannot be used to defend conditions which prevent the trial process from providing a fair and reliable determination of guilt. [381 U.S. at 583.]

The touchstone and the goal we seek to reach is, by the adoption of certain controls, to preserve a proper balance between the free flow of information and the maintenance of the integrity of the judicial process. That is what this Final Report is about. It is our thesis that such a balance can only be attained by the proper operation in unison of the component parts of the judicial establishment. Once the Bar and the police have formulated and enforced forthright and appropriate ethical standards and regulations to prevent leaks of information that very probably will prejudice the right to a fair trial, and the courts and the judges have adopted supplemental rules and practices to tighten up the methods of selecting juries and controlling trial procedures, we are confident that the present excesses will be greatly reduced and the cooperation of the news media more generously forthcoming. We perceive no reason why the preservation of the integrity of the judicial process should in any undesirable way interfere with or obstruct the free flow of the information and the commentary the public is legitimately entitled to expect from a free press.

Frank S. Hogan agrees that a high priority should be given to the implementation of the recommendations made in this report. He is in complete accord with the Committee's conclusion that the courts and the judges, the lawyers and law enforcement officials should make every reasonable effort to insure a fair trial. However, he does not agree with the opinion expressed herein that the First Amendment precludes a consideration of direct control of the news media, either by legislation or by expanded utilization of the Court's contempt power. He believes and has stated publicly that carefully and specifically drawn legislation could be enacted which would not offend constitutional limitations. The enactment of such legislation and greater use of existing contempt powers, he feels, should be endorsed by the Committee as a supplement for its other recommendations and for those cases where reliance on self-restraint proves futile.

In the following pages, the Committee has undertaken to analyze the role of lawyers, the police, and the judges and the courts in the Free Press and Fair Trial dilemma.

II

THE LAWYERS AND RECOMMENDED NEW CANON 20

THE cry against "trial by newspaper" or by radio or television is an old story. From the Supreme Court on down to John Doe, "trial by newspaper" is condemned. The place for the trial is in the courtroom, and all concerned in the process of deciding particular cases are supposed to be influenced only by the testimonial and documentary proofs admitted into evidence, the arguments of counsel, and the law as expounded by the trial judge. So much for theory. The true facts, as set forth in our Interim Report, *Radio, Television, and the Administration of Justice: A Documented Survey of Materials,* however, are that there is a wild scramble to get favorable publicity, and those leading the procession, more often than not, are the lawyers, including the prosecutor and his assistants, defense counsel in criminal cases, and lawyers for both sides in civil cases. And this is true despite the fact that the number of lawyers who act in this manner is extremely small. The great majority of the lawyers in the United States not only refrain from such practices but vigorously oppose them as detrimental to the best interests of the community and as a very real threat to the fair and impartial administration of justice.

It is likely that many were surprised or even shocked to read the quotations from 1 Am. Jur. Trials, entitled "Controlling Trial Publicity" (Interim Report, pp. 112-13) and the account of the daily television broadcasts from the steps of the courthouse by defense counsel during the trial of the alleged kidnapers of Frank Sinatra, Jr. (Interim Report, pp. 43-44). But it has become almost commonplace in sensational trials for murder, rape, and other crimes involving sex and violence to meet with such a barrage of press conferences, press releases, and appearances over the radio and on television—relating to the merits of the case, what witnesses will or will not testify, and the prior convictions and prior offenses of the accused—as to saturate a whole community and make the task of selecting truly impartial jurors difficult if not impossible. At times, as in the case of Francis Bloeth (Interim Report, pp. 50-54), where alleged insanity was involved, it is difficult to determine whether the prosecution or defense counsel and those associated in one way or another with the defense were more eager to advise the public of Bloeth's extraordinary career in crimes of violence that had preceded the murder with which Bloeth was charged. What occurred before and during the trial of Jack Ruby for the murder of Lee Harvey Oswald is still fresh in the minds of those who followed the case. Finally, the recital of what the lawyers did in the *Sheppard* case (Sheppard v. Maxwell, 384 U.S. 333), contained in the opinion of Supreme Court Justice Clark handed down so recently as June 6, 1966, can leave no doubt in the minds of reasonable men that something must be done to curb and, if possible, eliminate this tendency of some lawyers to try their cases in the newspapers or over the radio or on television.

FAILINGS OF CANON 20

The logical way to find a remedy is to look into the past and to try to find the reasons for the present unsatisfactory state of affairs. We start with Canons 5 and 20 of the Canons of Professional Ethics of the American Bar Association, adopted August 27, 1908.

5. The Defense or Prosecution of Those Accused of Crime

It is the right of the lawyer to undertake the defense of a person accused of crime, regardless of his personal opinion as to the guilt of the accused; otherwise, innocent persons, victims only of suspicious circumstances, might be denied proper defense. Having undertaken such defense, the lawyer is bound, by all fair and honorable means, to present every defense that the law of the land permits, to the end that no person may be deprived of life or liberty, but by due process of law.

The primary duty of a lawyer engaged in public prosecution is not to convict, but to see that justice is done. The suppression of facts or the secreting of witnesses capable of establishing the innocence of the accused is highly reprehensible.

20. Newspaper Discussion of Pending Litigation

Newspaper publications by a lawyer as to pending or anticipated litigation may interfere with a fair trial in the Courts and otherwise prejudice the due administration of justice.

Generally they are to be condemned. If the extreme circumstances of a particular case justify a statement to the public, it is unprofessional to make it anonymously. An *ex parte* reference to the facts should not go beyond quotation from the records and papers on file in the court; but even in extreme cases it is better to avoid any *ex parte* statement.

On January 25, 1957, Canon 20 of the New York State Bar Association was amended to read:

20. Press releases; any public statements by lawyers

It is unprofessional for a lawyer to make, or to sanction the issuance or use by another of, any press release, statement or other disclosure of information, whether of alleged facts or of opinion, for release to the public by newspaper, radio, television or other means of public information, relating to any pending or anticipated civil action or proceeding or criminal prosecution, the purpose or effect of which may be to prejudice or interfere with a fair trial in the courts or with due administration of justice. The foregoing shall not be applicable to publications or statements made in Court or to quotations from public records of the Court, or from depositions, or filed or served pleadings, or affidavits filed or submitted to the Court.

However, this canon shall not be so construed as to limit the right of an attorney in good faith to divulge information for publication in reply to any public statement which adversely affects the interest of his client, provided that the information is supported by facts, and does no more than contradict or mitigate the effect of said statement.

Enforcement

When the loopholes in the above quoted canons are taken into consideration, it need cause no surprise to find that these canons have been ineffective. By an impartial survey of major metropolitan areas as well as small towns and cities, we have discovered what appears to be an almost total lack of enforcement of Canon 20. As far as we have been able to ascertain, not a single lawyer has been disbarred, suspended from practice, or publicly censured for violation of Canon 20. The extent to which attorneys have been privately censured must, of course, remain uncertain but the instances cannot have been numerous. In the past six years, four attorneys—three defense lawyers and most recently a public prosecutor—have been privately censured for violation of Canon 20 after hearings before the Committee on Grievances of The Association of the Bar of the City of New York. But still there was no referral to the Appellate Division of the New York Supreme Court for disciplinary action. It should be noted, however, that the small number of complaints against prosecutors or their assistants in the First Department is due in large measure to the long-standing policy of District Attorney Hogan in New York County prohibiting his office from releasing confessions and other statements of those accused of crime.

And yet the instances are legion, and well known to the public, in which prosecutors have leaked to the news media alleged confessions, statements that a case is "open and shut," and full details of evidence that has not yet been presented in court. Certain defense counsel have persisted in trying their cases in the press and over the radio and on television. The ever-growing mass of literature on the Free Press and Fair

Trial issue is replete with examples of defense counsel outdoing prosecutors in calling news conferences for the purpose of obtaining publicity favorable to their clients. Even in those numerous instances when the accused or friends or the family of the accused has made statements to the news media, one must wonder to what degree these interviews and appearances over the radio and on television are instigated by defense counsel.

Escape Clauses

What makes the ABA Canon 20 of dubious value in curbing this abuse is that it is only applicable to newspaper discussion of pending litigation "generally," and publicity is allowed "in extreme circumstances." Thus there are exceptions, but what the exceptions mean would seem to be left to the imagination or judgment of the lawyer who resorts to the public forum. Moreover, violations of the spirit of Canon 20 have continued unpunished for so many years as to make court proceedings of questionable effect unless Canon 20 is drastically amended.

The loophole in the 1957 Canon 20 of the New York State Bar Association is in the last paragraph which apparently permits any kind of press release, press conference, or appearance on radio or television by a lawyer "in reply to any public statement which adversely affects the interest of his client." Moreover, the effectiveness of even the first paragraph depends upon the manner in which it is interpreted, as it refers only to actions "the purpose or effect of which may be to prejudice or interfere with a fair trial in the courts or with due administration of justice."

At first blush, it may seem reasonable enough to permit a lawyer to fight fire with fire, but a moment's reflection will make it apparent that even the publication of an indictment may be thought to justify defense counsel in publishing his version of the merits, what defense witnesses will testify, and so on. Once the interchange of publicity has begun, there is no way to stop it or in many if not most cases even to tell when or how it began.

The lack of enforcement of Canon 20, however, is not, in

the opinion of the Committee, due exclusively to the vagueness of its above-described versions. There is a tendency of the public and of courts and bar association grievance committees to view with some indulgence what may be mere "overzealousness" on the part of a prosecutor "honestly" seeking to put criminals in jail or on the part of defense counsel doing his utmost to extricate his client from the toils. In addition, in one of the bar association committee reports it is said: "Apparently publicity for upstate district attorneys and certain lawyers seemed to be a valuable political or business asset." This observation may well be applicable to certain types of lawyers everywhere.

HISTORY OF REVISION

Numerous bar association committees and other groups have been working for a considerable period of time in an effort to come up with a new Canon 20 that would effectively proscribe publicity by lawyers in connection with the trial of civil and criminal cases. For example, the American Bar Association *Coordinator,* for January 1966, cites programs of action by the Philadelphia, Florida, and Ohio Bar Associations. At page 3 of this issue of the *Coordinator* is the following description of the endeavors of the Ohio State Bar Association to enforce the existing ABA Canon 20:

The OSBA Committee on Legal Ethics and Professional Conduct earlier this year warned Ohio lawyers that Canon 20's restrictions on comments on pending cases will be strictly enforced.

In support of this program the OSBA public relations office will maintain a file of crime and trial news stories for use in investigating complaints against lawyers or newspapers alleged to have been the source of prejudicial statements or news stories. William Moore, assistant secretary and public relations director, said the file will be available to local bar associations for their use in dealing with both attorneys and newspapers.

In 1954 the Committee on the Bill of Rights of The Association of the Bar of the City of New York completed a five-year study of the sundry problems of Free Press and Fair Trial. In that Committee's Report to the Association, entitled "Report on Published Comment on Pending Litigation and Proposed Amendment to Section 20 of the Canons of Professional Ethics," the following extensive guidelines were set forth from which it was suggested an effective canon could be drafted:

We believe that members of the bar have a duty to refrain from originating the same types of statements which we believe should not be originated by or appear in the press, or otherwise be published. Such types of statements in relation to criminal proceedings, include statements of any of the following:

(a) Any criminal record of the accused;

(b) Any alleged confession or admission of fact bearing upon the guilt of the accused;

(c) Any statement of any constituted authority as to the guilt of the accused;

(d) Any statement of his personal opinion as to the guilt of the accused;

(e) Any statement that a witness will testify to certain facts;

(f) Any comment upon evidence already introduced;

(g) Any comment as to the credibility of any witness at the trial; and

(h) Any statement of matter which has been excluded from evidence by the court at the trial.

In relation to civil proceedings, such types of statements include statements of any of the following:

(a) Any statement of his personal opinion as to the merits of the claims of the plaintiff or defendant;

(b) Any statement that a witness will testify to certain facts;

(c) Any comment upon evidence already introduced;

(d) Any comment as to the credibility of any witness at the trial; and

(e) Any statement of matter which has been excluded from evidence by the court at the trial.

While the specificity and general merit of these guidelines did not result in any immediate amendment of Canon 20, a Special Committee on Amendment of the entire Canons of Professional and Judicial Ethics (of the ABA) is now in the process of preparing an entirely new set of canons.

On May 26, 1966, the New York State Bar Association Committee on Professional Ethics submitted to the ABA Special Committee just referred to a draft of a proposed new Canon 20 and a report, containing the following statement:

There is an irreconcilable difference between lawyers, including certain members of our Committee, as to what revisions, if any, should be made in Canon 20. One group would make it abundantly clear that the courtroom, and only the courtroom, should be the forum for the trial of civil and criminal cases, and that any participation by a lawyer for a party, by a prosecutor, or by a judge, in press releases or public statements to the radio, television or other news media is professionally reprehensible. Others feel that it is the right and duty of a lawyer to reply to publicity which adversely affects the interest of his client.

As pointed out by Dean Griswold in the Panel Discussion referred to below, the Standing Committee on Professional Ethics of the ABA has recommended an amendment of Canon 5 by adding the following new paragraph:

It is the duty of a lawyer engaged either in the prosecution or the defense of a person accused of a crime to refrain from any action which might interfere with the right of either the accused or the prosecuting governmental entity to a fair trial. To that end it is improper and professionally reprehensible for a lawyer so engaged to express to the public or in any manner extrajudicially any opinion or prediction as to the guilt or innocence of the accused, the weight of the evidence against him or the likelihood that he will be either convicted or acquitted.

As Dean Griswold states: "As far as this goes, it is laudable," but it "does not go nearly far enough," as the basic objection is to "the making of any sort of statement whatever about any pending criminal case."

Another approach, following the lead of the New Jersey

Supreme Court in State v. Van Duyne, 43 N.J. 369, 389 (1964), *cert. denied,* 380 U.S. 987, cited with apparent approval in Justice Clark's opinion in the *Sheppard* case above referred to, is to interpret the existing ABA Canon 20 so as to proscribe most of the prejudicial publicity by lawyers. This method has been elaborated in State v. Trantino, 43 N.J. 211 (1965), and State v. Thompson, Minn., 139 N.W.2d 490 (1966). A similar approach has been followed by the Executive Committee of The Association of the Bar of the City of New York in the following statement appearing in the Association's official publication, 21 *Record* 355 (June, 1966):

Statements to the Press—Canon 20

For the past several years serious questions have been raised by the public and the bar concerning statements made to the press or through other news media by lawyers involved in civil litigation or criminal proceedings that appeared to prejudice the litigant's right to a fair trial or otherwise interfere with the due administration of justice.

Such statements are contrary to both the spirit and letter of Canon 20 of the Canons of Professional Ethics and, on occasion, have resulted in a complaint of unprofessional conduct before the Association's Committee on Grievances.

Canon 20 of the New York State Bar Association's Canons of Professional Ethics (the Canons which serve as a guide to the courts of the State of New York in disciplinary proceedings) provides:

"Press Releases and Public Statements by Lawyers

"It is unprofessional for a lawyer to make, or to sanction the issuance or use by another of, any press release, statement or other disclosure of information, whether of alleged facts or of opinion, for release to the public by newspaper, radio, television or other means of public information, relating to any pending or anticipated civil action or proceeding or criminal prosecution, the purpose or effect of which may be to prejudice or interfere with a fair trial in the courts or with due administration of justice. The foregoing shall not be applicable to publications of statements made in Court or to quotations from public records of the Court, or from depositions, or filed or served pleadings, or affidavits filed or submitted to the Court. However, this canon shall not be so construed as to limit the right of an attorney in good faith to divulge information for publication in reply to any public statement which adversely affects the interest of his client, provided that the information is supported by the facts, and does no more than contradict or mitigate the effect of said statement."

The Executive Committee is of the opinion that a lawyer's conduct must at all times conform to the standards of the legal profession as set forth in the Canons of Professional Ethics, including Canon 20. The Committee, moreover, is convinced that the organized Bar must assume the initiative in preventing all incursions on the right of litigants, whether civil or criminal, to a fair trial by reason of any departure from the prohibitions of Canon 20.

To this end the Executive Committee calls attention to types of statements made by attorneys out of court that may interfere with the fair trial or otherwise prejudice the due administration of justice and which are, therefore, prohibited by Canon 20. Such statements include, but are not limited to:

1. Statements concerning the merits of the claims of a plaintiff or defendant in a civil action, or the guilt or innocence of a defendant in a criminal proceeding.

2. Statements concerning the existence or contents of confessions or admissions of a defendant in a criminal proceeding.

3. Statements concerning testimony or other evidence to be introduced in a civil action or criminal proceeding.

4. Statements concerning testimony or other evidence which has been excluded by the Court in a civil action or criminal proceeding.

5. Statements concerning the conduct, reputation or criminal record of any party or witness in a civil action or criminal proceeding.

6. Statements of opinion concerning rulings by the Court in a civil action or criminal proceeding.

The Executive Committee also calls attention to the fact that four of the Association's committees are actively co-operating toward amplification of the prohibitions of Canon 20. In the meantime, the Bar is reminded that strict compliance with the letter and spirit of Canon 20 is the personal obligation of every lawyer.

In the opinion of the Committee the drastic amendment of Canon 20 is a more forthright and effective way to deal with the problem under discussion. We should frankly face the fact that a factor that has undoubtedly operated to inhibit forceful policing of violations of at least the spirit if not the very terms of Canon 20 is the sorry record of the past inactivity of the organized Bar. It is time to make a fresh start.

It would be tedious and unprofitable to make reference to the large number of other bar association reports and proposals for the amendment of Canon 20. It is the old story: Whenever lawyers embark upon some much needed reform in the administration of justice, the fundamentals are obscured by a host of differences, some of substance, but most of them relating to phraseology and details. In such a maze the focal issue of "trial by newspaper" becomes enmeshed and obscured in a mass of verbiage that contributes little if anything to the solution of the very pressing problems of Free Press and Fair Trial.

PRINCIPLES OF REFORM

The Committee finds no legal or other obstacle to the formulation of ethical standards of conduct for lawyers, who are at all times officers of the court and subject to discipline for acts and statements detrimental to the fair and impartial administration of justice. Nor has the Committee any doubt that the sort of publicity described in its Interim Report and proscribed by the terms of its proposed new Canon 20, below, is harmful and prejudicial to the due and proper administration of justice.

The Committee's theory is widely supported by legal scholars of the highest caliber. At a Panel Discussion at the American Bar Association Convention in New York City on August 11, 1964, as part of the Law-Layman Program conducted by its Section of Judicial Administration, on the subject "The Right of Fair Trial: Responsibility of the Public, the Legal Profession, and the News Media," Dean Erwin N. Griswold of the Harvard Law School, said:

The Canons should be amended to include an absolute prohibition on the release by any lawyer, either for the prosecution or for the defense, of any material relating to the trial, either before the trial, or while the trial is going on. This should specifically preclude appearances of any sort on radio or television relating to the forthcoming or pending trial. It should also specifically forbid the release of any statements to the effect that the defendant has or has not confessed, or that he has or does not have an alibi, or otherwise. It should also specifically preclude the release of evidence which would be inadmissible in court, or the release of evidence which has been offered in court and excluded by the trial judge.

In its comprehensive study of the subject in hand, this Committee has attempted to reach its own conclusions independently of others in the hope that its recommendations for action thus independently formulated may be of greater value.

Thus, before we set forth our own version of what should be the wording and substance of the new Canon 20, we have unanimously agreed upon the following underlying principles:

1. Civil actions and proceedings and criminal prosecutions should be tried in a courtroom and not in the newspapers, over the radio or on television.

2. The professional and ethical standards relevant to the subject of "trial by newspaper" or over the radio and on television should be expressed in simple, clear, and specific terms.

With these principles in mind we recommend that Canon 20 be amended.

RECOMMENDED NEW CANON 20

A. It is unprofessional for a lawyer publicly to make, or sanction the publication or broadcast of, an out-of-court statement or disclosure of fact or opinion regarding a pending or anticipated civil action or proceeding or criminal prosecution. It is therefore the ethical responsibility of lawyers to refrain from the public issuance of statements or other disclosures relating to such action, proceeding, or prosecution, which concern:

1. The merits of the claims of a plaintiff or defendant in a civil action or proceeding, or the guilt or innocence of a defendant in a criminal prosecution;
2. The existence or contents of a party's confession, admission, or other pre-trial declaration;
3. Testimony or other evidence to be offered at trial;
4. Matters of fact bearing upon the cause, which will not be offered in evidence at trial;
5. The credibility or reliability of witnesses, or the probative force of other evidence offered or to be offered at trial;
6. Testimony or other evidence which has been excluded by the court;
7. The conduct, reputation or criminal record of any party or witness;
8. The rulings or decisions of the court during the litigation;
9. Any other matter which may tend to interfere with a fair trial, or may otherwise tend to prejudice the due administration of justice.

B. It is the duty of a lawyer engaged in a civil action or proceeding or a criminal prosecution to attempt to restrain his client and witnesses from making any out-of-court statement or disclosure of fact or opinion proscribed by this canon.

C. The foregoing, however, shall not be deemed to restrict the issuance of a brief statement by a lawyer concerning:
1. His client's intention to plead not guilty in a pending criminal prosecution, or to defend a pending civil action or proceeding;
2. The identity of the defendant in a pending criminal prosecution or the fact, the time and the place of his arrest, or the charge or charges against him;
3. The identity of the parties to a pending civil action or proceeding, the claim asserted and the amount in controversy.

III

POLICE AND OTHER LAW ENFORCEMENT AGENCIES AND RECOMMENDED CODE OF REGULATIONS

JUST as we have already said that no complete or satisfactory solution of the Free Press and Fair Trial dilemma is possible without the voluntary cooperation of the news media, we repeat that no such solution is possible without the voluntary cooperation of the police and other law enforcement agencies. Just as the First Amendment prevents effective measures against the news media, so does the absence of any adequate power in the courts, vis-à-vis the police and other law enforcement agencies, prevent the discipline of the police except by the operation of procedures established within the framework of particular police departments in particular localities. We treat this subject in some detail, especially with reference to the powers of trial judges, in Chapter IV of this Final Report concerning the courts and the judges.

POLICE PRACTICES TODAY

We have catalogued in our Interim Report sufficient illustrative instances of conduct by officials, including the police, concerned with the administration of criminal justice regarding release to news media of information which tends to defeat those ends of justice concerned with the right of a defendant to a fair trial. We did this to demonstrate the need for some regulation of law enforcement officials. It should now be clear that disclosure to and publication by news media—whether by newspapers, periodicals, radio, television, or by other means—of a defendant's criminal record, interviews with the accused, the existence or the details of an alleged confession, evidentiary details which led to his arrest, or comments or opinions concerning his guilt tend to reduce the probability of trial by an impartial jury, competent to arrive at a verdict solely on the basis of testimonial and documentary proofs received in evidence at the trial.

Pressures for Disclosure

The Committee is well aware of the forces which lead police agencies into patterns of full disclosure to news media. Even more than with other governmental service organizations, the police are required by the community to demonstrate constantly and concretely their capacity to fulfill their responsibilities, among which the protection of society from criminal conduct ranks foremost. Specifically, when crimes of violence occur, in particular those of murder, assault, rape, and robbery, creating widespread apprehension and at times holding the community in a grip of terror, the public demands to know what is being done to apprehend the perpetrators. To some extent, the responsibility for not having prevented the crime is placed at the doorstep of the police, whether it occurred in a public place, in a private dwelling, or in a commercial establishment. The community grows increasingly restless and concerned as the interval between commission and apprehension lengthens. Pressure begins to build up for concrete indications that the case is nearing solution and that the perpetrator will soon be in custody, so that the fears of the community may be allayed. When concrete assurances are not forthcoming, confidence in the competence of the police force weakens, and, in some instances, insinuations or accusations of nonfeasance or malfeasance begin to develop and to gain momentum. Statements from police officials to the effect that the investigation continues with diligence and efficiency do little to satisfy the community's anxiety to know the specifics of the progress.

The Reaction by the Police

The news media, which consider themselves spokesmen and representatives of the public, press a relentless search for full details, most of which are within the knowledge of law enforcement agencies. And the police, anxious to avoid a running battle with newspapermen, unfair critical editorial comment, and general ill-will, are tempted into premature and prejudicial releases. To avoid the accusation of suppressing information which might tend to cast the police in an unfavorable light, some departments have adopted an "open door" policy to news media and permit them wide access to reports and personnel.

In any event, when success, measured by police in terms of arrest, crowns their efforts, law enforcement agencies are eager to share it fully with the community. Every effort is made to set at rest any doubt that the defendant is the perpetrator. In recent months, as well-publicized instances of "false confessions" have instilled doubt and suspicion in the minds of a substantial segment of the public, the latter consideration has assumed more significant proportions. To dispel these attitudes and to demonstrate their competence, law enforcement officials have disclosed many details of the case against the defendant, including eyewitness identification, fingerprint evidence, and his prior criminal record.

As a related part of this search for public confidence, the police have attempted to show that their efforts to prevent crimes are weakened to a substantial degree by the high rate of recidivism. By releasing the defendant's criminal record they, in effect, argue that, notwithstanding their best efforts in the past, some other branch of the criminal justice system has granted him the freedom to prey once again on the community.

Thus, it has been the aim of police agencies to gain or regain the confidence and support of the public. The police seek this support not merely for its own sake but also because it is their judgment that the apathy on the part of many members of the community toward crime may be reduced by the restoration of respect for the police as a crime-fighting organization. Thus in an interview following his installation, Police Commissioner of the City of New York Howard Leary was quoted as saying:

> If there is any censorship of news media it shouldn't be done by police. The Police Department needs the press. The press is in a sense for our protection. It's the only way for the Police Department to tell its story without sermonizing or lecturing. [New York *Herald Tribune*, February 23, 1966.]

THE NEED FOR CHANGE

Clearly there is merit in the position taken by the police. Through its research this Committee believes it has acquired some understanding of the problems which beset law enforcement agencies and a considerable sympathy with the efforts of the police to deal with these problems. Nevertheless, the simple and inescapable fact is that the fair administration of criminal justice is suffering from the present course of police conduct. The courts have emphatically and repeatedly held that the present practices tend to prejudice the defendant's right to a fair trial. Without that constitutional protection, society is ultimately the victim.

It is incumbent on the police and law enforcement agencies to adhere to standards which today either have not been formulated or are not being followed. While other levels of the criminal justice system, including the judiciary, the prosecutor, and defense counsel, may be directly supervised and controlled by the courts, the police are relatively independent of these controls, a subject we discuss more fully in Chapter IV, "The Courts and the

Judges." The probability of effective, uniform legislation is remote and unrealistic.

Thus, it is essential to an over-all improvement that the police reevaluate their existing procedures and adopt stringent self-regulatory codes. We have documented in our Interim Report at pages 117-43 the remarkably divergent policies followed by police organizations throughout the country. Some departments have little or no formal criteria governing the dissemination of information to news media. Others, while professing to maintain standards, have promulgated regulations too broad and too general to be of concrete value. Our recommended code contains unambiguous directions to police agencies. We hope these proposed regulations will serve as workable guidelines, satisfying the conflicting needs of the defendant, the police, the community, and the news media.

In the formulation of the Proposed Code for Police and Law Enforcement Agencies, the text of which appears at the end of this chapter, we have endeavored to weigh the conflicting needs of all, but the overriding consideration which has guided us is the protection of the constitutional rights of the defendant. Only where a clear and urgent law enforcement purpose exists or where the probability of prejudice is remote or nonexistent may the release of more than a brief, general description of the crime and of the accused be justified.

We recognize that the adoption of a police code cannot be a cure-all for the improper release and publication of prejudicial matter. Many items which we recommend be barred from release by police may be in the public domain or otherwise readily available to newsmen. Court records or newspaper files of previous cases involving the defendant may contain his criminal and personal history; talkative witnesses, anxious for the limelight, may fill in many gaps in the full account of the crime and the defendant's role; shortsighted police officers may "leak" information anonymously. Indeed, in the face of the ingenuity of the press, which is legend, little can remain the confidential property of official law enforcement agencies for too long a period of time. Thus our efforts cannot be successful unless the news media accept a higher degree of responsibility, similar to that which we are hereby recommending for the police.

Moreover, it will be difficult for law enforcement officials to adhere to any code unless the public, as well as the news media, is educated to accept silence by the police, not as a sign of ignorance but as basic to the protection of the constitutional rights of the accused. The public must learn to accept the principle that, under due process, the proper forum for disclosure is the trial and that when the police refuse to reveal their evidence, to make the defendant available at the time of apprehension for press interviews and photographing or to answer the multitude of searching questions posed by news media, it is for the protection of society, not of themselves.

Furthermore, it is the responsibility of the organized Bar to rally to the aid of police administrators when the pressures for full disclosure begin to build. If the Bar will add its considerable prestige and influence in support of law enforcement's efforts to protect the rights of the defendant to an impartial trial, the police will be better able to withstand those pressures.

RECOMMENDED CODE FOR POLICE AND LAW ENFORCEMENT AGENCIES

A. Concerning the Defendant

1. The release of information concerning the defendant shall be limited to his name, age, occupation, marital status, and personal data not related to the crime or the character of the defendant. His criminal record, prior medical and psychiatric history, or military disciplinary record, if any, shall not be released. No other information that is clearly prejudicial to the defendant shall be released.

2. No statement of any nature made by the defendant, or the

substance thereof, shall be released. No reference shall be made to any test taken by the defendant or that he has refused to take.

3. The announcement of the arrest of the defendant may include, in addition to the information authorized in paragraph A.1, the time, place, and manner of apprehension, as well as the text or summary of the charge, information, or indictment. No comments shall be made relating to his guilt or innocence.

4. News media shall not be permitted to interview the defendant, with or without his attorney's consent, while he is in police custody.

5. News media shall not be permitted to photograph or televise the defendant while he is in police custody and in other than a public place. This prohibition extends to such instances as where he is being interrogated, where he is being processed ("booked") following arrest, where he is in a lockup or detention facility, or where he is at a hospital bedside for identification purposes. The defendant shall be escorted through public places as expeditiously as possible. While the news media shall not be prevented from photographing or televising the defendant in a public place, he shall not be halted or posed for their convenience.

6. Where the defendant is still at large, and it appears that he is a fugitive from justice, additional information that may reasonably and directly aid in effecting his apprehension, including his photograph, may be released.

B. Concerning the Crime, the Investigation, and the Arrest

1. A general description of the crime shall be made available to the news media. Gruesome or sordid aspects which tend unduly to inflame public emotions shall not be released. Witnesses shall not be identified by name or otherwise, nor shall any comment be made concerning their credibility, their testimony, or their identification of the defendant.

2. Wherever possible, the taking of photographs of maimed or deceased victims shall not be permitted.

3. No comment on the apparent motivation or character of the perpetrator shall be made.

4. No information concerning scientific evidence such as laboratory or ballistics tests or fingerprints shall be released.

5. At the time of arrest, in addition to the information which may be released concerning the defendant, the announcement may include the identity of the investigating and arresting officers, and the time duration of the investigation.

C. General

1. A member of the police agency shall be designated as the Information Officer responsible for the dissemination of all information to the news media. It will be the responsibility of the Information Officer to supervise the enforcement of these regulations and to solicit and encourage full cooperation of news media. No member of a police agency may furnish any information to news media without prior approval by the Information Officer. No interviews shall be permitted with investigating or arresting officers.

2. Wherever feasible, the Information Officer will encourage news media to enter into pool arrangements so as to reduce confusion and interference with the orderly processes of law enforcement. It shall be a prime responsibility of the Information Officer to insure a calm and orderly atmosphere during the dissemination of information to news media.

3. The above regulations are to be adhered to even in those instances where charges of police inefficiency or misconduct appear in the public press or where the published reports are misleading or inaccurate. It shall be the obligation of the Information Officer to refuse to elaborate on the information previously released under this Code, except in those circumstances where the correction of false publication may serve to assist in the apprehension of the defendant or will not prejudice his right to a fair trial. The failure on the part of others to maintain adequate stand-

ards will not justify avoidance by police agencies of their responsibilities to insure the ends of justice.

THE OUTLOOK FOR CHANGE

As with the news media so with the police and law enforcement agencies there are almost day-to-day developments in the direction of a more realistic attitude toward publicity that may be prejudicial to defendants in criminal cases. Only as recently as October 10, 1966, the Kentucky State Police Director and the Louisville Public Safety Director agreed to join with an existing state press–bar committee to establish voluntary guidelines for reporting crime news.

We do not expect our proposed Code of Regulations for Police and Law Enforcement Agencies to be adopted out of hand. But we hope it may be received in the spirit with which it is offered, that is, as an ideal toward which progress may be made and as suggestive of specific phases of the subject that deserve further discussion and inquiry.

IV

THE COURTS AND THE JUDGES

THE prospect of the tightening up of old procedures and the development of new ones by the courts and the judges to prevent or at least measurably to curtail prejudicial publicity is promising. Notable instances of mass publicity and a general "carnival atmosphere" have in the past stirred the conscience of the public, as in the Hauptmann and Hall-Mills cases, but this soon abated and in trials involving "murder and mystery, society, sex, and suspense" things went from bad to worse. An example of this is clearly presented in *The Trial of Jack Ruby* (1965) by John Kaplan and Jon R. Waltz, published by Macmillan. The announcement of Justice Clark's opinion in the Supreme Court, on June 6, 1966, in the case of Sheppard v. Maxwell, 384 U.S. 333 (Justice Black dissenting, without opinion), however, ushered in a new era. This Supreme Court decision, including the footnotes, is annexed to this Final Report as an Appendix. It is well worth extended and careful study by all those interested in the subject of Free Press and Fair Trial. All of the opinions of the various members of the Supreme Court, including the footnotes, in the prior case of Estes v. Texas, 381 U.S. 532 (1965), appear in full in our Interim Report, *Radio, Television, and the Administration of Justice* (1965), at pages 192-250.

The judgment and philosophy underlying the *Estes* and *Sheppard* decisions and the touchstone of our position is that the courts have the necessary power to assure a fair trial free from the effects of prejudicial publicity and that the courtroom, courthouse premises, and participants in a trial—whether they be parties, witnesses, jurors, attorneys, court and police officials, or news media personnel—are, in varying degrees, subject to the exercise of that control by the trial judge.

Trial judges have the authority and the responsibility to take measures to insure a fair trial. A fair trial demands, in addition to other factors, freedom from prejudicial publicity and an orderly and dignified courtroom atmosphere. The trial judge is the central figure in the operation of every trial. It becomes his responsibility, therefore, to control the participants in the trial and all activities in and about the courtroom during a trial.

Against this background we shall endeavor to analyze various separate features of the general problem and to discuss each of these in some detail. It is well to bear in mind, however, that we have found little decisional law to guide us. Our comments and our reasoning, however, cover many practical details of considerable importance. These comments may be helpful to readers generally, whether lawyers or laymen, and to the Judicial Conference of the United States or its Committees or similar state bodies in the event that consideration is given to the implementation by rules of court of the trial judge's powers to control prejudicial publicity, referred to in Justice Clark's opinion in the *Sheppard* case. It is of special interest that Chief Justice Warren has recently appointed a new committee of the Judicial Conference of the United States "On the Operation of the Jury System," headed by Circuit Judge Irving R. Kaufman. Among other things this committee will "set up guidelines to shield Federal juries from prejudicial publicity."

Moreover, our discussion of the various "orders" and other "directions" that may be made by the trial judge in the exercise of his power to control "the integrity of the trial" is based on what we think is the necessary assumption that the trial judge has power also to enforce and to punish deliberate and willful conduct in flagrant disobedience of such "orders" or other "directions." Furthermore, when infraction is immediate or nearly so and its deliberate character is manifest, prompt action would seem to be required if the judge's control of the trial is not to be irretrievably lost.

PRETRIAL PUBLICITY

The Courthouse and Its Personnel

Having said that the trial judge can and should do much to protect the trial from prejudicial publicity and to insure an orderly trial free of circus or carnival atmosphere, we are not unmindful that much prejudicial matter may occur before a case reaches any courtroom or judge and that much that may occur to prejudice a party in a criminal case is beyond the constitutional control of any of the judges. But courthouses and their environs, court clerks, bailiffs, and other court personnel are clearly within the ambit of court rules and other similar regulations, applicable generally or to certain local judicial establishments, according to the federal or state background. Our Interim Report at pages 145-92 contains the text of certain of these rules applicable to the federal courts and to various state courts with respect to the taking of photographs. Our continuing investigation, however, has disclosed numerous instances where photographs have been taken and published in violation of these rules and there appears to have been little or no effort to enforce them or to discipline the violators. To the extent that this laxity is due to a lack of precise and clear enforcement procedure it would seem that the existing rules should be amended or supplemented by the setting up of some simple enforcement procedure defining the duties of those who are to prosecute the violators and the powers of particular courts or other officials of the particular judicial establishment in question to initiate and prosecute disciplinary measures.

If necessary, which we doubt, new rules could readily be formulated to prevent leaks and other disclosure of information by marshals, deputy marshals, court clerks, bailiffs, and other court personnel. In such cases we have no doubt of the power of the various courts to establish proper controls to be enforced by the judges themselves.

During the Pretrial Period Should the Courts and the Judges Impose Controls on the Police, the Lawyers, and the Press?

As usual there is, on the one hand, the question of power or jurisdiction and, on the other hand, the question of policy. Moreover, one cannot consider the two questions *in vacuo*. They must be discussed in relation to the groups of persons who would be affected by the control of prejudicial publicity. Thus, starting with the commission of the crime or the arrest of the accused or the filing of the indictment or information and continuing up to the time of the commencement of the trial or thereabouts, it is a serious question, both of power and of policy, whether the court in which the case is to be tried, or any court, should, by rule of court, by authority of legislative enactment, or by virtue of some competence supposed to be inherent in the judicial function, have the right, vis-à-vis lawyers, members of the police force, or representatives of the press, to proscribe the publication or utterance of matter deemed prejudicial to the right of the accused to a fair trial. If such right exists, either actually or *in ovo*, then the judges, in this pretrial period, must have the power to fine and imprison as for contempt of court all lawyers, members of the police force, and representatives of the press who violate the orders or rules of proscription. The prospect, in this pretrial period, of judges of various criminal courts of high and low degree sitting as petty tyrants, handing down sentences of fine and imprisonment for contempt of court against lawyers, policemen, and reporters and editors, is not attractive. Such an innovation might well cut prejudicial publicity to a minimum. But at what a price!

Initially a distinction must be drawn within the word "pretrial" between the purely investigatory stage before any judicial proceeding has been instituted and the second stage which begins when the defendant is brought before a commissioner or magistrate or when a grand jury proceeding has commenced. The Committee is firmly of the opinion that the courts lack any power whatsoever over the police or the news media during the first stage of the pretrial period, except the ever-present power to control activities in and around the courthouse.

During the second stage, the authority of the court increases to encompass those judicial or quasi-judicial proceedings. Regarding the grand jury, for example, the court has a measure of control similar to its control over the trial and petit jury. Thus the court has the power to control the physical activities in and about the jury room and will administer an oath of secrecy the violation of which is a contempt. Similarly, the court's control over witnesses, prosecuting attorneys, and other participants in grand jury proceedings is analogous to its authority over participants in the actual trial—a subject examined below in some detail.

Nevertheless, with respect to the police and the press in the entire pretrial period we think it unwise and detrimental to the public interest to give such contempt powers to the courts and the judges. Moreover, we think that such proceedings and the court rules, legislation or what not else authorizing such contempt proceedings might well be held to be a violation of the First Amendment guarantees of free press and free speech. Furthermore, as to the police, we find no authority inherent in the courts or the judges to discipline them for alleged breach of their duties as police officers.

There is a great variety of statutes, municipal ordinances, and miscellaneous orders having the force of law, the general effect of which is to place control of the police force or other law enforcement officials in the hands of a chief of police or police commissioner, subject to certain powers of appointment and removal in the mayor or other municipal or village or county executive. In certain localities officials who perform duties similar to those of the police are part of the staff of the district attorney or prosecutor. We are not aware of any direct general relationship between the police and the courts. It would thus seem that the only way to prevent leaks and the large number of other prejudicial practices in the pretrial period, illustrated in our Interim Report, at pages 25-32, *passim*, is by the adoption and enforcement of some such voluntary code as we recommend in Chapter III of this Final Report. Ordinances and legislation or quasi-legislative controls do not seem to us to be desirable because of their rigidity and for other reasons.

But there have been gropings in the direction of an extension of the power of trial judges over the police or the formulation of a new gloss on existing law. Thus the Criminal Court of Baltimore at one time promulgated Rule 904, following, which has since been repealed:

In connection with any case which may be pending in the Criminal Court of Baltimore or in connection with any person charged with a crime and in the custody of the Police Department of Baltimore City or other constituted authority, upon charges of crime over which the Criminal Court of Baltimore has jurisdiction, whether before or after indictment, any of the following acts shall be subject to punishment as contempt. . . .

(C) The issuance by police authorities, the State's Attorney, counsel for the defense, or any other person having official connection with the case, of any statements or admissions made by the accused, or other matters bearing upon the issues to be tried.

In addition, Rule 904 prohibited the publication of any of the matter covered by the text of the rule. The first contempt citations under this rule were secured against various members of the news media. The Maryland Supreme Court, reversing these convictions, held that, in order to sustain the convictions, a clear and present danger to the administration of justice must be shown, and that it had not been shown. Baltimore Radio Show v. State, 193 Md. 300, 67 A.2d 497 (1949), *cert. denied*, 338 U.S. 912 (1950). As we have already stated in Chapter I of this Final Report, "The First Amendment," at pages 5-6, this is the case in which Justice Frankfurter filed his eloquent dissent.

Two state courts of last resort, in New Jersey and Minnesota, have addressed themselves to the subject of the general powers of courts or judges to control the police in connection with allegedly prejudicial publicity in criminal cases, and each of these courts has denied the existence of any such power. In State v. Van Duyne, 43 N.J. 368, 204 A.2d 841 (1964) it was said that the matter is "largely in the hands of the prosecutor and local police authorities." In State v. Thompson, 139 N.W.2d 490 (Minn. 1966), the court remarked: "Police officers, over whom we have no such disciplinary power, ought likewise to be dealt with by their superior officers." 139 N.W.2d at 514. It is also of more than passing significance that Justice Clark in *Sheppard*, Appendix, p. 92, stated:

Being advised of the great interest in the case, the mass coverage of the press, and the potential impact of publicity, the court could also have requested the appropriate city and county officials to promulgate a regulation with respect to dissemination of information about the case by their employees.

On the other hand, as reported in the New York *Times* on September 18, 1966, Superior Court Judges Mallard and Braswell, at a trial term in Wake County, North Carolina, issued the following order:

After arrest and before final determination in this court of any criminal case which may come before it, no accused, counsel, prosecutor, witness, law enforcement officer, court staff, court official, or any person engaged in or assisting in the investigation, preparation, or trial of the case shall make any statement for the purpose of publication, or having reason to believe that it will be published, concerning the fact of or contents of any confession or statement of the accused, or concerning any prior criminal record of the accused, or the fact of or the results of any tests, or what the evidence is expected to be, or comment upon the credibility of any witness, or express any opinion as to the guilt or innocence of the accused.

The *Times* also reported general compliance on the part of the local police.

The extent to which this sort of muzzling of the press and of everyone else can be projected is illustrated by an order made on August 9, 1966, by a judge in the Twentieth Judicial District Court for the State of Colorado. A coed had been brutally murdered on the campus of the University of Colorado. While the police sought to withhold prejudicial information from reporters, the case was featured in the local press for several weeks. The day following the filing of charges against a suspect, and on motion of the district attorney, the following order was made in People of the State of Colorado v. Joseph Dyre Morse, Criminal Action No. 4090:

THIS MATTER coming before the Court upon the motion of the District Attorney, the Defendant not appearing in person but by and through his attorney, Rupert M. Ryan, who expressly waived the presence of the Defendant, and the District Attorney's Office being present by Rex H. Scott and Joseph C. French, and the Court having considered the motion,

IT IS ORDERED that the People's Motion Be Granted To Prohibit Extra-judicial Statements From Officers of Boulder County Sheriff's Office, City of Boulder Police Department, City of Longmont Police Department, Adams County Sheriff's Office, All Those Witnesses Listed With the People's Information Heretofore Filed, and University of Colorado Officials and Employees save and excluding, however, that the Defendant's attorneys, Rupert M. Ryan and Gerald A. Caplan or the District Attorney, Rex H. Scott, Assistant District Attorney, Joseph C. French, Captain Donald H. Vendel, Lieutenant Lowell D. Friesen, Bruce G. Denneny, Detective Clinton H. Fullen and Marvin Nelson be allowed to speak with all witnesses listed in the People's Information for purposes of preparing the case.

IT IS THEREFORE ORDERED that any person within the above described categories is hereby prohibited from revealing to any person, corporation or partnership including all news media with the exception as to those people above described any statements concerning any knowledge as to the facts in the above captioned case.

The Committee believes this order is a clear violation of the guarantees of free press and free speech contained in the First Amendment. It is an illustration of the lengths to which courts and judges would go in their endeavor to proscribe prejudicial publicity if in this pretrial period they had the power to do so. That such orders could be used to cover up incompetence, venality, and a deliberate but covert desire to impede or frustrate criminal procedures against guilty politicians or those involved in racial disputes and other violence seems to us to be apparent on the face of the matter.

With respect to lawyers, who are officers of the court, there may well be a residue of power in the courts to formulate rules or issue orders proscribing the making of public allegedly prejudicial statements by lawyers and authorizing contempt sentences of fine and imprisonment for violation by lawyers of the rules or orders. Here again, as in the case of the police, and irrespective of the question of power, we think such an innovation unwise and we recommend against its adoption. The traditional way to discipline lawyers for wrongful conduct and unethical practices detrimental to the administration of justice is by proceedings for disbarment, suspension from practice, or censure, initiated by Bar Associations and presented to courts of competent jurisdiction for adjudication. In states with an integrated Bar the procedure is somewhat different but substantially the same in essence. As we have already pointed out in Chapter II, the reasons for the lack of prosecution of lawyers for improper publicity in the past have been many and various, but principally the looseness of phraseology and the lack of specificity in ABA Canon 20. We do not favor the creation by court rules or otherwise of alternate or additional remedies in the pretrial period by the imposition of fines and prison sentences on lawyers by courts or judges for contempt of court. On the other hand, we would not alter or diminish existing traditional contempt powers against lawyers for serious misconduct having a prejudicial effect on the administration of justice.

Miscellaneous Proceedings That May Be Conducted in Camera

In the opinion of the Committee a great variety of miscellaneous proceedings, to which the Sixth Amendment guarantee of a public trial does not apply and to which various state statutes, court rules, and practices requiring proceedings to be public, directly or by implication, do not apply, fall into the same category and are governed by the same rules. Although controlling authority is lacking we think the subject too important to be passed over without comment. We refer to conferences and arguments in the judge's chambers or the robing room between the lawyers and the judge on matters of practice and procedure, involving questions of law and not going to the merits. On these occasions the judge is not required to admit either the public or the press. But if he does admit the press the proceeding is, in our opinion just as public as if the hearing was open to all. If the judge thinks it best to avoid the possibility of prejudicial publicity, all he has to do is to exclude all persons except the lawyers and others who are to participate in the conference. But if, in the exercise of his discretion, he admits representatives of the press, then the hearing is public in the same sense that the trial itself is public, and the judge has no power to proscribe the publication by the press of an account of what occurred at the hearing. He may advise, exhort, beg and beseech, or attempt to persuade the press not to publish, and he may succeed. But if he makes an oral or written order not to publish, this Committee is of the opinion that the First Amendment as interpreted by the Supreme Court bars punishment of the newsman or editor for disobedience of the order. And we think this is as it should be.

Proceedings in Open Court

When matter that might be prejudicial to the rights of a defendant is brought to light in open court during a trial or other proceeding, but in the absence of the jury, the same principle must apply. "A trial is a public event. What transpires in the court room is public property." Craig v. Harney, 331 U.S. 367, 374 (1947). In many instances it is highly desirable that the news media not publish or broadcast what the judge has already ruled should not be brought to the attention of the jurors. We hope that the codes, statements of principles, and guidelines formulated and to be formulated by the press on a voluntary basis will specifically include this particular matter. But, the plain fact is, in our opinion, that the judge has no power to order the news media not to publish and he has no power to punish an editor or broadcaster for contempt for the disobedience of such an order.

For example, our Interim Report documents several instances where both state and federal trial judges have, during criminal trials, orally issued blanket orders to the press such as the following: "don't print anything that is said in open court—even though it goes into the trial record—in the absence of the jury." Interim Report, pp. 62-63.

In a slightly different context the same principle is illustrated by a decision of the Supreme Court of Arizona, handed down on October 5, 1966, in Phoenix Newspapers, Inc. v. Superior Court, Doc. No. 8713. Just prior to the selection of jurors for his trial on the charge of first degree murder the defendant obtained a hearing on a petition for habeas corpus. After the judge found that probable cause had existed for the defendant to be bound over for trial, the defense successfully moved for an order barring any publication by the press relating to the hearing. Here is Judge Thurman's ruling:

We have here a man who is going to be tried for homicide. The County Attorney is going to ask for the death penalty. I don't want the newspapers to publish what happened here this morning. The jury will be selected this afternoon at 2:30 p.m., and if any of this matter is presented in the presence of anyone outside, I will find that individual or individual of the press in contempt of this Court.

Despite the order, the Phoenix *Gazette* published a factual account of what occurred in open court at the hearing. Contempt proceedings followed and the Supreme Court of Arizona issued a Writ of Prohibition against them. The opinion for the Court, written by Chief Justice Struckmeyer, construing and applying the free press provisions of the Arizona Constitution, reviews the cases in some detail and understandably reaches the conclusion: "The restraint imposed by the trial court in this case strikes at the very foundation of freedom of the press by subjecting it to censorship by the judiciary."

Just the same there is much to be said in favor of Judge Thurman's remark: "if it is published that I found probable cause . . . it would be tantamount to everybody reading the paper to believe that he is already guilty." It is at such times as this that the community should be able to rely on some measure of voluntary restraint by the news media.

Summary

Adoption of our recommendations for the drastic amendment of Canon 20, as described in Chapter II of this Final Report, and our recommended Code of Regulations for Police and Other Law Enforcement Agencies, as described in Chapter III, should eliminate much of the prejudicial pretrial publicity. But, in the opinion of the Committee, during the pretrial period the news media are restrained only by their own voluntary act from publishing information independently discovered by private persons, and protected by the First Amendment.

AN ORDERLY AND DIGNIFIED COURTROOM ATMOSPHERE

A fair trial becomes more and more unlikely as the physical arrangements in and near the courtroom lead to noise, confusion, and overcrowding. These arrangements are always within the sole control of the trial judge. If the defendant and his counsel are huddled into a small and inadequate space in such proximity to representatives of the news media that conference between counsel and client without being overheard is all but impossible and private notes and documents, whether or not already received in evidence, may be read and even handled or photographed by representatives of the news media, constant objections and protests are to be expected. If television apparatus, cables for radio communication, and a host of telephones are permitted in rooms adjacent to the courtroom or to the jury room, and reporters and others are constantly hurrying here and there, the calm and dignified atmosphere so essential to the conduct of judicial proceedings becomes impossible to maintain. The news photographers have become an unmitigated nuisance. If not restrained, they pounce upon all the participants in the trial, including not only the lawyers and the defendant and his family but prospective witnesses and others coming in and out of the courtroom. All this can readily be avoided by appropriate directions given by the trial judge. He alone must bear the blame for the confusion and disorder and the consequent stream of prejudicial publicity.

Indeed, as we have already said in connection with the taking of photographs, and despite the written rules of court barring broadcasting in or near the courtroom set forth in Chapter IV of our Interim Report at pages 144-92, our research has disclosed repeated violations of these rules, in various parts of the United States. Perhaps this is because there seems to be no person specifically designated to enforce these rules. Certainly it is not to be expected that a trial judge who countenances such open and notorious flouting of the rules will discipline himself.

Thus it is incumbent upon the judge or the appropriate judicial council or conference to establish permanent and precise rules governing the access of the public, most especially including the press, to all areas of the courthouse—jury rooms, witness rooms, corridors, and entrances, as well as the courtrooms. Similarly precise rules should be made to control the conduct of members of the news media, whether the court is in session or has recessed, especially concerning photographs and interviews. Courthouse personnel should be instructed not only regarding the enforcement of rules relating to courthouse conduct but also concerning their personal conversations with newsmen.

In any trial that has attracted more than normal publicity, the trial judge must be prepared to issue more detailed instructions regulating those persons who are to be admitted to the courtroom to prevent overcrowding and the movement in and about the courtroom to prevent undue distractions while the court is in session.

At this point a few general observations may be in order. Judges like others in various professions and occupations vary greatly in disposition and temperament. Moreover, in many instances the situation suddenly and unexpectedly gets out of hand. At least the disgraceful scenes in Dallas police headquarters after the assassination of President John F. Kennedy, portrayed so graphically in the Warren Commission Report, all pertinent parts of which are reprinted in our Interim Report at pages 302-17, and what occurred at and after the trial of Jack Ruby for the murder of Lee Harvey Oswald, together with the bare facts related in Justice Clark's opinion in *Sheppard v. Maxwell,* Appendix at pages 70-82, have alerted the public to the abuses and derelictions incident to massive publicity. We think that the judges themselves will on their own initiative take proper measures to avoid such "Roman holidays" in the future.

It may be mentioned in passing that it does not seem wise to assign the trial of a sensational case to a judge who will come up for reelection shortly after the termination of the trial.

POWERS OF THE TRIAL JUDGE VIS-À-VIS
DIRECT PARTICIPANTS IN THE TRIAL

We have already treated in some detail the strict clear and present danger test applied in First Amendment cases affecting out-of-court publications by the news media, that is, giving the free press feature of the First Amendment "the broadest scope that could be countenanced in an orderly society," or "the broadest scope that explicit language, read in the context of a liberty-loving society, will allow." But the common-law powers of the trial judge to punish those who violate his orders directly affecting matters of trial administration and courthouse procedure are not governed by this strict clear and present danger test. There is a discussion of this distinction in Brumfield v. State, 108 So. 2d 33 (Fla. 1959). And, even if the clear and present danger test is applicable, we think that the violation of orders made at the trial to preserve "the integrity of the trial" meets that test as a matter of law. Appendix, pp. 88-92.

Where one of the direct participants in the trial willfully disregards an order by the trial judge not to discuss the case with representatives of the news media or to make other public out-of-court statements and the order is necessary or appropriate in the particular case to keep publicity under control, we believe that the trial judge has and ought to have power to adjudge such person in contempt. The connection of these groups of persons with the trial itself is too intimate and close to admit any other conclusion.

We have already treated the subject of marshals, deputy marshals, court clerks, bailiffs, and other court personnel.

The Selection and Control of Jurors

The most prejudicial effect of inflammatory publicity is upon the minds of jurors and prospective witnesses. Our Interim Report contains numerous documented illustrations of instances where on the *voir dire* jurors have withheld the facts concerning their reading of prejudicial matter, listening to radio commentators, or viewing television where the guilt or innocence of the accused is under discussion. There are instances of flagrant disobedience by jurors of instructions by the trial judge not to have any contact with such publicity during the trial.

There is at least one case where the trial judge instructed the jurors that they had a right to read, listen to, or view anything they chose, but that they must disregard such publicity when arriving at their verdict. Interim Report, p. 61. In another instance, despite instructions, one of the jurors brought a transistor radio into the jury room and the jurors listened to comments about the trial over the radio during their deliberations on the subject of the guilt or innocence of the accused. Interim Report, p. 68.

In numerous instances the interrogation of the jurors by the trial judge on the *voir dire* was perfunctory and inadequate. At times the trial judge was satisfied of the competency of jurors even though they remained silent and made no response to his questions. There was a widespread tendency to rely on a final general statement by a juror that he could put prejudicial matter out of his mind and render a just verdict on the proofs adduced in open court supplemented by the argument of counsel and the instructions of the court, even if the juror had previously testified that he read much of the adverse publicity and came to the trial thinking the defendant guilty. Many appellate courts found such statements sufficient to establish the impartiality of the juror, relying on the fact that the trial judge had an opportunity to observe the demeanor of the juror and had exercised his judicial discretion in refusing to excuse the juror. It is our recommendation that appellate courts generally should follow the lead of the Supreme Court in *Sheppard* and "make an independent evaluation of the circumstances" when the competency of jurors is attacked on the review of a judgment of conviction. Appendix, pp. 92-93.

Admittedly the subject is a difficult one. Some measure of discretion must be held to reside in the trial judge. It is not practical to have an incisive and really penetrating examination of one juror in the presence of the other members of the panel sitting in the courtroom listening. At the same time one must recognize that in connection with the great bulk of trials there is no massive publicity. Where the trial has become a *cause célèbre,* however, and the question of the extent to which the minds of the prospective jurors have been affected by inflammatory publicity of one kind or another is of paramount importance, it is our recommendation that the *voir dire* examination be made of each prospective juror separately and not in the presence of the other jurors on the panel from which the petit jury is to be selected.

This interrogation of individual jurors separately, however, is part of the "public trial" guaranteed by the Sixth Amendment and the trial judge may do no more than suggest or request the representatives of the news media to refrain from publicizing the examination of the individual jurors, as such publicity would be likely to come to the attention of those prospective jurors who had not already been examined and selected or rejected as jurors.

On the other hand, at the moment the panel of jurors is sworn, its members become a part of the judicial establishment and subject to control by the courts. When the panel is sworn, the jurors should receive firm instructions not to communicate with anyone concerning any aspect of any case with which they come in contact. These instructions should emphasize that questions asked on *voir dire* are included and that conversations with members of the news media are absolutely prohibited.

Once the challenges have been disposed of and the jury and alternates, if any, selected and sworn, it is of the utmost importance that some way be found to impress upon the mind of each juror that it is his or her solemn duty during the entire course of the trial to refrain from reading anything in the newspapers about the trial or to listen to radio broadcasts about it or look at television when the trial is being commented upon. As it may be assumed that, except where state laws require it, juries will generally not be sequestered, and practically every home is equipped with one or more radios and television sets about which members of the family cluster to look and listen, nothing short of a very good conscience and earnest and repeated instructions by the trial judge will suffice to keep a juror insulated. Perfunctory instructions seem clearly inadequate. As a matter of emphasis, each juror, before the taking of testimony or the opening statements of counsel, might be required to sign under oath a written statement containing a solemn promise not to read or listen to newspaper, radio, television, or other stories or comments concerning the trial. It should be possible for trial judges to explain, without giving the slightest offense to juries, what might be the possible effect on the trial of a violation of this pledge.

It is clear to us that a juror who disobeys such instructions is guilty of contempt of court and, whenever such delinquency is disclosed, should not be permitted to depart unscathed.

A more difficult question relates to the power of the trial judge after the jury's verdict has been rendered and the jury polled to direct the jurors not to talk to the news media about how they voted, the nature of their deliberations, or other matters connected with the trial. An a fortiori illustration is presented when, the jury having disagreed, or for other reasons, a mistrial is ordered. As a judgment of conviction may be reversed and a new trial ordered by an appellate court and, in the event of a mistrial, there again may be another trial of the issues, it would seem to be obvious that widespread publication of the votes of the jurors, their deliberations, and how they stood from time to time before the rendition of the verdict or the declaration of a mistrial would be highly prejudicial, to either the defense or the prosecution. This is a situation that should be clarified. Regardless of such limitations on the trial judges as may be found to exist with respect to such instructions, in any event, his powers of moral suasion can be most effective. In one case that was widely publicized the trial judge obtained a solemn promise from each juror not to discuss the case and this procedure was effective. The following day the forewoman of the jury, a worker in a beauty shop, telephoned the trial judge and said that a representative of a magazine offered a large sum of money for an interview. Reminded of her promise, the juror refused the interview.

We have already mentioned certain matters with respect to which we think the news media have failed to give to the administration of justice the voluntary cooperation that this Committee expects from a great institution like the press. The publication of the names, addresses, and photographs of the jurors in a sensational trial is in this category. It may well be true that the names and addresses are usually matters of public record. Energetic newsmen and broadcasters can always dig out photographs and miscellaneous news items about the jurors and their families, their mode of life, and just about everything else about them. If such information is published or broadcast by the news media the inevitable result, as stated by Justice Clark, in his *Sheppard* opinion, Appendix at page 85, is to thrust the jurors "into the role of celebrities" and expose them "to expressions of opinion from both cranks and friends." That it will interfere with the proper performance of their duties as jurors is manifest. The trial judge can do something to insulate the jurors from reporters, it is true. But it would be a big help if the news media voluntarily refrained from publishing names, addresses, and other details.

Parties

PARTIES TO A CIVIL ACTION. A plaintiff, having voluntarily submitted himself to the jurisdiction of a court, and a defendant, brought under such jurisdiction by service of process or by voluntary appearance, are bound to submit to all lawful orders of the court or its judges. The Federal Rules of Civil Procedure leave no doubt on this point and the same is true generally throughout the United States under Civil Practice Acts and Rules. Thus, if a party to a civil action gives tangible evidence of a propensity to go beyond the exercise of his First Amendment rights and to bring pressure to bear upon a judge or jury by trying his case in the newspapers or over the radio or on television, the court has power, from the very time jurisdiction over the person has attached to the entry of judgment, to order such party to desist. This is because such conduct plainly has a prejudicial effect on the administration of justice in the particular case. Occasion for the use of such orders in civil cases is rare, but not unprecedented. Interim Report, pp. 105-13. More often than not the offender is one of the lawyers or both. Various sanctions are available for purposes of enforcement.

DEFENDANTS IN CRIMINAL CASES. Whether in custody or enlarged on bail a defendant in a criminal case does not forfeit any of his constitutional rights, including those arising under the First Amendment. Thus he may make a statement to the newspapers or others declaring his innocence. But he has no right to bedevil the processes of justice by pouring forth during the progress of the trial a variety of inadmissible and prejudicial matter at a series of press conferences and television appearances, as was done by Mrs. Candace Mossler during her trial on the charge of having murdered her husband, as described in Chapter V of this Final Report, "Recent Developments." In Chapter II, our proposed new Canon 20 imposes upon counsel the duty "to attempt to restrain his client and witnesses from making any out-of-court statement or disclosure of fact or opinion proscribed by this Canon."

In a trial that might result in a judgment of death or long imprisonment it may well be that a defendant would be willing to take the risk of a sentence for contempt as the price of obtaining a jury biased in his favor. It is believed, however, that the lack of authority on the subject is due in no small measure to the fact that the inflammatory publicity is generally harmful rather than helpful to the defendant, and, in any event, he is not likely to disobey instructions and take on the onus of such sanctions as might be imposed upon him by the trial judge.

Witnesses

It is significant that Justice Clark places witnesses in the same category with lawyers, parties, and court officials, all of whom may be said to be closely connected with "the integrity of the trial." Appendix, pp. 91-92. He comments that the trial court might well have proscribed extrajudicial statements by any lawyer, party, witness, or court officials who divulged prejudicial matter. There would seem to be no difficulty with a contempt proceeding against a person under subpoena who had notice of an order not to make any statements out of court except to counsel and not to read or listen to reports of the trial, but who willfully disobeyed the order. The efficacy of a blanket direction to witnesses is presently being tested in many courts. Perhaps a rule of court might be formulated and a copy of this rule printed on the subpoenas.

If it is thought necessary to insulate witnesses, either for their own protection or to avoid the confusion and distraction of repeated questionings by various persons, the traditional, but seldom applied remedies are the sequestration of the witness or a direction that he may not testify at all. These remedies do not seem practical or desirable when numerous persons are potential or prospective witnesses and the context is that of a highly publicized trial.

Police and Other Law Enforcement Officials

While Justice Clark's opinion in *Sheppard* states that the trial judge should have "made some effort to control" the release of information to the press by "police officers, witnesses, and the counsel for both sides" and also speaks of "imposing controls" over statements to the press "especially" by the "Coroner and police officers," Appendix at pages 91-92, elsewhere in the opinion, as already noted, it is said that the trial judge could have "requested the appropriate city or county officials" to regulate the remarks of their employees. Appendix, p. 92.

Thus, we think, the power of control to be exercised by the trial judge over the police, and related government officials such as a coroner, is the same as the power of control over the witnesses. When certain particular police officers have had such a close and intimate relationship to the trial that they may be said to be part of the trial itself, then they come within the area of control. Otherwise, the "integrity of the trial" cannot be maintained. As the body of law affecting the preservation of the constitutional rights of those accused of crime enters into a new development, we have no doubt that the subject will be further clarified by judicial decisions and, perhaps, by the formulation and adoption of new rules.

CONTINUANCE, CHANGE OF VENUE, SEQUESTRATION, MISTRIAL, AND REVERSAL

The rules governing these remedies are well established. Whether or not they are to be applied in particular cases is and must remain largely a matter of the discretion of the trial judge. More and more, however, appellate courts have felt it their duty to do what Justice Clark, in his opinion in *Sheppard*, calls making "an independent evaluation of the circumstances," instead of rubber-stamping the order of the trial judge as an exercise of discretion. There is need for more of this appellate "independent evaluation of the circumstances," especially in connection with the selection of jurors. While reversals, as Justice Clark says, "are but palliatives" and the expense of new trials is a high price to pay for the exuberance of the news media and the questionable practices of many of their informants, to say nothing of the possibility that in the end a person guilty of some monstrous crime may be freed again to prey upon the community, the salutary effects of the *Sheppard* reversal are already manifest. Moreover, it is only by reading the details set forth in the masterful, closely reasoned opinion of Chief Justice Warren in the *Billie Sol Estes* case, our Interim Report at pages 204-28, and in Justice Clark's opinion in *Sheppard,* that the public can be made aware of the cumulative effect of massive, prejudicial publicity and the fact that it is a menace to the administration of justice. Indeed, had the Supreme Court taken the *Hauptmann* case on certiorari and reversed for a new trial, describing the "circus" and "Roman holiday" features of that famous trial, it is not likely that the situation would have become as bad as is reflected in our Interim Report.

A trial judge is always reluctant to declare a mistrial, for much the same reasons behind the reluctance of appellate courts to reverse and order a new trial. Sometimes, however, it is difficult to see any other alternative.

Sequestration of jurors is, in theory, an ideal remedy for publicity appearing during the trial and has long been the practice in a very few states in certain types of cases. There are many objections to sequestration based upon practical considerations such as expense and inconvenience. In criminal conspiracy cases, many of which consume from four to twelve months of the time of all concerned, it would seem that the hardship to jurors would be too great. That sequestration should be ordered more frequently than in the past, however, is the conclusion reached by this Committee. Whether it should be compulsory or in the discretion of the trial judge, however, must depend largely on local conditions and on this subject the Committee expresses no opinion.

V

RECENT DEVELOPMENTS

THE long history of abuses in the area of trial publicity which justified the existence of this Committee persists. The continuing prejudicial effect of pretrial and trial reporting is the most forceful argument for the adoption of the recommendations presented in this Final Report. The Committee's Interim Report, *Radio, Television, and the Adminstration of Justice,* presented documented examples of how the news media may improperly influence the minds of prospective and actual jurors and witnesses. Since the publication of that report by the Columbia University Press in 1965, waves of literature about the Free Press and Fair Trial dilemma have appeared. Meanwhile, the Committee has continued to observe and collect newspaper, radio, and television stories about criminal and civil litigation. This collection shows only too clearly the pressing need for corrective measures.

PREJUDICIAL PUBLICITY

While there appears to have been some alleviation of the prejudicial tone of these reports and some striking but isolated improvements, the Committee has found that many stories possessing unfair, prejudicial, and inflammatory matter continue to appear in the news media. The lack of progress in the area of prejudicial news releases stands in contrast to the advances made in other areas touching on the rights of the accused to a fair trial. For example, when a man was arrested for the murder of eight student nurses in Chicago, the police were scrupulous in observing the rules laid down by the Supreme Court in *Escobedo* [378 U.S. 478 (1964)] and *Miranda* [384 U.S. 436 (1966)], but seemingly paid no attention to the principles in the *Estes* and *Sheppard* cases. Thus, for example, the police released the criminal record of the accused and his identification by an eyewitness. Furthermore, the local chief of police publicly announced that he was "absolutely positive" of the guilt of the accused.

Because the end product of a prejudicial story is the printed page or the airwave, it is perhaps too easy to place blame on the news media. The Committee fully realizes that much of the objectionable material which reaches the public is instigated by or obtained through the cooperation of the lawyers and the police. Nevertheless, it is equally certain that many stories are originated, and others inflated, by the newsmen themselves.

The Press

Newspaper reports containing matter which perhaps all would agree is prejudicial continue to occur daily. In many instances, however, reporters have not been satisfied with publishing only those materials which have been made available but have sought out, often at great effort, persons involved in the event, seeking additional and perhaps conflicting information. The following examples are illustrative:

On October 25, 1965, the New York *Journal-American* printed an article under headline: " 'Turnstile Justice' 7 Arrests . . . and Probation." The article went on to relate what it called "another chapter of the story of 'turnstile justice' in which hardened dangerous criminals are given a 'slap on the wrist' by lenient judges and allowed to go free to continue their criminal pursuits." During the course of the story, the accused's prior criminal record was mentioned several times in such language as: "a record of seven arrests"; "ex-convict"; "three jail terms"; "arrest record dates back to 1954." Additionally, the following was printed:

A puzzling aspect of the case . . . came to light when the Journal-American applied at the office of [the] Deputy Police Commissioner . . . for the ex-convict's record.

"Can't give it to you," said a lieutenant. "[An] Assistant District Attorney . . . has ordered [the accused's] . . . record to be withheld." . . . But reporters have other ways to get information for the heavy file of "turnstile justice." Here is the police record.

The newspaper then proceeded to recite with full details the prior record of the accused. See also the New York *Journal-American* of January 27, 1966, for a story dealing with a young suspect accused of arson who recanted his confession. The reporter assigned to this story wrote that the accused had again admitted his guilt to a private individual after he had recanted to the police authorities.

The Broadcasters

Nor have the actions of the broadcasting media personnel improved significantly. On February 7, 1966, at 11:00 P.M. a major local television station, in New York, broadcast an interview with the officer who had arrested a dope addict accused of killing his girl friend by giving her an overdose of heroin. During the interview, the officer said that at the time of the accused's arrest "his speech was incoherent and his eyes glassy." The officer also made the point several times that heroin was found in the possession of the defendant.

Another major local station at 11:00 P.M. on January 17, 1966, carried an interview of a television newsman with a defendant accused of murder. It appeared that the accused had signed a confession and had later disavowed it. In the original confession there were statements that the deceased female had scratched the accused's face in the course of a struggle. The interviewer asked how he could account for the fact that he presently had scratches over his face. When the accused tried to brush-off the subject, the newsman persisted in this line of questioning.

Of course, some media of public information on occasion do demonstrate restraint in publishing or broadcasting criminal news. Often a newspaper will not print certain information at the request of the police in order to aid them in apprehending a suspect. And while it is not precisely a recent development, it is of particular interest that on June 10, 1964, at the request of prosecuting authorities, a producer for the Columbia Broadcasting System "blacked out" certain parts of California to prevent viewers from seeing a television broadcast which involved a case that was pending in the "blacked out" locale. See 39 *Journal of the State Bar of California* 743 (1964). Such responsible behavior is indeed praiseworthy.

Grand Juries

Nor have news media personnel ceased trying to invade the secrecy of grand jury proceedings. A story appearing in the March 31, 1966, edition of the New York *Times* told how a federal grand jury in Chicago was forced to move the location of its proceedings because of the glare of publicity caused by over-curious newsmen. Similarly, public officials have not ceased to encourage widespread publicity about grand jury proceedings. A classic illustration can be found in the investigation conducted in the late summer of 1966 into wrongdoing at the New York State raceways. Press coverage of the proceedings was extensive and clearly abetted by the officials in charge of the investigation. Ultimately, on September 13, 1966, the presidents of the three tracks took a full-page advertisement in the New York *Times* urging District Attorney Koota to "Get the guilty parties and stop making a production out of it." Thereafter, the quantity of publicity which accompanied the investigation subsided. Also, in the New York *Times* of September 28, 1966, there were charges by the New York Civil Liberties Union that when several alleged Mafia leaders were "detained" by police and subpoenaed for questioning before a grand jury, the "familiar burlesque performance" was "conducted as a sort of running press conference in utter contempt for judicial rulings on pretrial publicity" and "staged when one of the principals is running for election."

There are many reasons why a trial may become the object of prejudicial publicity. Counsel may seek it or some unusual aspect may catch the eye of a reporter. And when the proper combination of sex and violence is present, the case may descend into the realm of the true carnival. That such sensationalized trials can still occur despite the growing consensus that they must be outlawed was amply demonstrated in January, 1966, when Mrs. Candace Mossler and Melvin Lane Powers were tried in Florida for the murder of Mrs. Mossler's husband. Press coverage was intense throughout the trial with interviews given inside the courthouse and even in the courtroom "at every recess." On numerous occasions, the presiding judge himself was interviewed by the press. The events in Florida well illustrate what may always be the case; in order for the news media to accumulate sufficient information to keep the reading public interested, they must have the cooperation of the participants in the trial. Here is was perfectly clear that Mrs. Mossler herself was a most willing source of sensational publicity. For example, on January 19, 1966, at 11:15 P.M., the New York station of a major television network broadcast an interview with Mrs. Mossler, who speculated that her husband died at the hands of a jealous male lover since he had been indulging in homosexuality several months prior to his death. There was a similar statement in the New York *Journal-American* of January 18, 1966. Thus *Time* Magazine of February 4, 1966, reported that

Some 40 reporters from around the U.S. were covering the trial last week, and some more are expected. . . . And Candy was taking no chances on reporters' losing interest; she regaled them with the sorrows of her life and with the peculiarities of her husband.

These reporters and commentators then had little to do but gather potentially prejudicial information for publication. *Time* Magazine documented this situation in its February 4, 1966, issue:

Searching for new angles, a few reporters concentrated on peripheral people. The Miami Herald's Gene Miller described prospective jurors, including an insect exterminator who was opposed to the death sentence for humans. Theo Wilson was impressed with a seeress named Jeannie, who turned up at the trial and claimed that she had never made a wrong prediction. Her verdict on Candy: innocent.

As they reworked the same material and rewrote the same leads, some reporters inevitably succumbed to the temptation to try the case prematurely in their columns. "Candy is positive that she had nothing to do with the demise of her rich old husband Jacques," wrote Bishop, who apparently disagreed with Jeannie. "She is equally positive that her sister's little six-foot boy Melvin had nothing to do with it. When one thinks of the 39 stab wounds sustained by Jacques, in addition to having a crystal flamingo broken over his head and the impact of a Coke bottle which fractured his skull, it is difficult to imagine a stranger applying himself with such diligence. Either way, the lawyers are going to cost half a million. Jacques Mossler may be in the awkward position of paying to spring his betrayers."

Whether the defendants in Florida, or the state, received a fair trial must be subject to serious doubt.

The fact that news people at times may be of assistance to the administration of justice is obvious. It cannot be doubted that in at least some of the illustrations set out above, the press believed itself to be acting in the public interest: either allaying the fears of the community or exposing official ineptitude of one sort or another. But on the whole, as indicated in our Interim Report, the price that society pays in terms of the deleterious effects on the legal process is high.

VOLUNTARY CODES

Fortunately, not all the developments since the publication of our Interim Report have been of the character above described. In some noteworthy instances, police and prosecutors have taken steps to avoid the release of prejudicial information and members of the news media have adopted voluntary codes or "guidelines" seeking to prevent the publication of such material. And in recent months the judges themselves have undertaken more frequently to prevent trial participants from granting interviews with the press and to dissuade the press from publishing prejudicial matter.

Our Interim Report at pages 277-79 set out the "guidelines" for crime reporting that had been adopted in 1965 by the Columbia Broadcasting System. The first steps in this direction taken by independent radio stations occurred in October, 1966, when four affiliated New York State stations adopted a code which was described as similar to the C.B.S. "guidelines." This radio code prohibits broadcasters from discussing criminal records or confessions unless, as is also the case under the Toledo *Blade* guidelines set forth below, "an overriding public need" requires that the information be made public. It is noteworthy that the president of the operating group, R. Peter Straus, in announcing the restrictions remarked that the stations had been experimenting with the code for a year and had found it successful. New York *Times,* October 3, 1966.

The most auspicious development came a month earlier when the Toledo *Blade* and the Toledo *Times* adopted a voluntary code which was developed with the cooperation of the Toledo Bar Association. Toledo *Blade,* August 21, 1966; New York *Times,* August 22, 1966. This code is reprinted here in full because of its importance. It stands as a perhaps unique acknowledgment by a leading newspaper that trial coverage has too often exceeded the bounds of propriety and that the news media themselves, in conjunction with local bar associations, are capable of ameliorating the situation.

Guidelines on Publicity in Criminal Proceedings

Recognizing the vital importance of the constitutional right to a fair trial, The Blade adopts the following set of self-imposed guidelines on publicity in criminal proceedings. It should be understood, however, that we also have other responsibilities under the Constitution and that these cannot be waived. The First Amendment guarantee of a free press, for example, imposes an obligation to guard the public interest in all phases of governmental activity. Thus, The Blade will always investigate thoroughly—with or without the cooperation of official agencies—any evidence of malfeasance, misfeasance or nonfeasance of anyone in public office.

And in pursuance of this responsibility, along with the obligation to help insure society at large as well as a defendant of the right to a fair trial, this newspaper may be required to alert the public or reassure the community beyond the limitations of these guidelines.

Thus, these guidelines might have to be modified, or specific limitations might have to be suspended under any of the following examples of abnormal circumstances:

A wave of violent crimes might so stir community apprehension that something more than limited information about law-enforcement activity would be required as a matter of assurance to the public.

A similar situation might arise if there were a real danger of a breakdown in law-enforcement. Or, there might be a lapse of conduct expected of a public official that could bring disgrace upon the office or the community. Also, modification of these guidelines might be required if a public official faced charges and there were efforts to shield him, or an investigation into official actions appeared to have bogged down.

Modified procedures also might be necessary if other sources of information so aroused the public through sensational reports—particularly from out of town—that this newspaper could not maintain its credibility without taking account of information or misinformation spread by others.

Except for the above qualifications, only the following information should be published in stories of criminal proceedings:

1. The name, age and address of accused person(s).
2. How the arrest was made, and when, and where.
3. The charge(s) against the accused person(s), and the identity of the complainant(s).

4. The fact that a Grand Jury has returned an indictment and that a trial date has been set.

5. Newsworthy trials will be covered in detail so that essential information may be conveyed to the public at a time when it will not interfere with the judicial process.

Unless very special circumstances dictate otherwise, as indicated above, the following types of information shall not be published in cases of criminal arrests:

1. Any prior criminal record of the accused.

2. Any so-called "confession" the accused may have made other than the fact that he has made a statement to police. But there shall be no indication of the nature of that statement.

3. Any statements by officials or others construed as detrimental or beneficial to the accused person.

4. Any statements by attorneys either detrimental or beneficial to the accused or concerning any defense that is to be made during trial.

5. Any names of jurors selected for a particular trial.

6. Any arguments made in court in the absence of the jury, or any evidence excluded by the court.

One of the conclusions reached by this Committee is that because of the principles embedded in the First Amendment, the conduct of the press is largely beyond the control of the courts and the judges. But the autonomy whch the Constitution guarantees the news media carries with it the responsibility for putting their own house in order. Thus the most helpful step which can be taken to promote impartial trials is for the news media to adopt voluntary codes covering all aspects of crime reporting. Hopefully, in taking this step, the press will accept, and will be offered, the advice and cooperation of all bar associations. The problems in this area vary somewhat in the different localities and there may not be any one "best" code. Rather, the local Bar working with the local news media may devise the code which best suits the needs of their community.

It is for this reason that the steps recently taken in Toledo and New York are of such importance. Hopefully, now that the ice has been broken, other news media and local bar associations will more easily adopt their own "guidelines."

It is almost of equal significance to the adoption of these codes that the Toledo *Blade* itself asserted that their "guidelines" could not be a final solution of the problem of conflicting values. In an editorial appearing on August 21, 1966, the *Blade* pointed out that the particular social institution which is a newspaper has traditions which are intrinsically counter to the protection of the accused. Thus, the editorial asserted that "the primary responsibility for protecting the rights of the accused rests with the legal profession. . . . If lawyers will conform to the spirit of their professional canons in pretrial statements to all media of information, our professional task as newspapermen will be greatly eased."

These entirely valid newspaper traditions plus what the *Blade's* editorial referred to as its "obligations to the community," compelled the Toledo papers to include a series of reservations in their code. Because of the breadth of these reservations, the rights of the accused will hang on the continued good faith of any paper which promulgates a code containing similar exceptions. And it cannot be doubted that the views and interpretations of the various members of the news media will vary widely. For example, could not the pretrial press coverage in the *Sheppard* case have been sought to be justified under the "breakdown in law-enforcement" clause? And, given the national scope of press coverage, would not the developments in any notorious case be considered by some to justify invoking the "taking account of information . . . spread by others" clause?

It is certainly not our desire to criticize the commendable steps taken in New York and Toledo. Rather, the Committee wishes to underscore what the *Blade* itself pointed out: it is the inherent tendency of the press to accumulate and print information and the rights of the accused cannot be properly protected until the judicial establishment cleans its own house.

THE ABA REPORT

We have read with great interest the Reardon Report of the ABA Advisory Committee on Fair Trial and Free Press which we consider a major contribution to this subject. The differences between us are not nearly so significant as our basic agreements. Both committees recognize that is is important to work out proper restrictions on lawyers, the police, and others who may make statements that could affect the fairness of the trial. We recognize both the inherent power of judges at the trial to impose proper restrictions on conduct in the courtroom or the vicinity that might affect a fair trial and the power to impose controls on the participants of the trial. The differences between us affect only the means and methods to be used to attain the ends we both have in view.

CONCLUSION

We conclude this Final Report with a feeling of optimism. At last the community at large, as well as the courts and the judges, the lawyers and the bar associations, and every segment of the news media, has been alerted to the dangers of prejudicial publicity. All must now recognize that "bedlam" and the "carnival" and "Roman holiday" aspects of sensational criminal trials are a disgrace to American justice. The continuing efforts by all concerned to improve the situation are most encouraging.

It is our belief that such reluctance as has been manifested by the news media is largely due to the fact that they have felt their independence and their First Amendment rights were under attack and in jeopardy. Once it becomes firmly established that these fundamental rights are not in jeopardy and that their contribution to the purification of the judicial process is a voluntary one, as we have sought in this Final Report to demonstrate, their cooperation will be more generously forthcoming. Moreover, the claim of the news media that the prejudicial publicity emanates largely from those connected in one way or another with the law enforcement agencies and others who are part and parcel of the judicial establishment and that the judicial establishment has not done what it should have done to correct these abuses, rests in a solid basis of fact. When we do our part, as we can and as we should, the dawn of a new day may be at hand.

And so, with a sigh of relief, we put our baby to bed.

APPENDIX

SHEPPARD v. MAXWELL
DECIDED JUNE 6, 1966
384 U.S. 333

Mr. Justice Clark delivered the opinion of the Court.

This federal habeas corpus application involves the question whether Sheppard was deprived of a fair trial in his state conviction for the second-degree murder of his wife because of the trial judge's failure to protect Sheppard sufficiently from the massive, pervasive and prejudicial publicity that attended his prosecution.[1] The United States District Court held that he was not afforded a fair trial and granted the writ subject to the State's right to put Sheppard to trial again, 231 F. Supp. 37 (D. C. S. D. Ohio 1964). The Court of Appeals for the Sixth Circuit reversed by a divided vote, 346 F. 2d 707 (1965). We granted certiorari, 382 U. S. 916 (1965). We have concluded that Sheppard did not receive a fair trial consistent with the Due Process Clause of the Fourteenth Amendment and, therefore, reverse the judgment.

I

Marilyn Sheppard, petitioner's pregnant wife, was bludgeoned to death in the upstairs bedroom of their lakeshore home in Bay Village, Ohio, a suburb of Cleveland. On the day of the tragedy, July 4, 1954, Sheppard pieced together for several local officials the following story: He and his wife had entertained neighborhood friends, the Aherns, on the previous evening at their home. After dinner they watched

---

[1] Sheppard was convicted in 1954 in the Court of Common Pleas of Cuyahoga County, Ohio. His conviction was affirmed by the Court of Appeals for Cuyahoga County, 100 Ohio App. 345, 128 N. E. 2d 471 (1955), and the Ohio Supreme Court, 165 Ohio St. 293, 135 N. E. 2d 340 (1956). We denied certiorari on the original appeal. 352 U. S. 910 (1956).

television in the living room. Sheppard became drowsy and dozed off to sleep on a couch. Later, Marilyn partially awoke him saying that she was going to bed. The next thing he remembered was hearing his wife cry out in the early morning hours. He hurried upstairs and in the dim light from the hall saw a "form" standing next to his wife's bed. As he struggled with the "form" he was struck on the back of the neck and rendered unconscious. On regaining his senses he found himself on the floor next to his wife's bed. He raised up, looked at her, took her pulse and "felt that she was gone." He then went to his son's room and found him unmolested. Hearing a noise he hurried downstairs. He saw a "form" running out the door and pursued it to the lake shore. He grappled with it on the beach and again lost consciousness. Upon his recovery he was laying face down with the lower portion of his body in the water. He returned to his home, checked the pulse on his wife's neck, and "determined or thought that she was gone."[2] He then went downstairs and called a neighbor, Mayor Houk of Bay Village. The Mayor and his wife came over at once, found Sheppard slumped in an easy chair downstairs and asked, "What happened?" Sheppard replied: "I don't know but somebody ought to try to do something for Marilyn." Mrs. Houk immediately went up to the bedroom. The Mayor told Sheppard, "Get hold of yourself. Can you tell me what happened?" Sheppard then related the above-outlined events. After Mrs. Houk discovered the body, the Mayor called the local police, Dr. Richard Sheppard, petitioner's brother, and the Aherns. The local police were the first to arrive. They in turn notified the Coroner and Cleveland police. Richard Sheppard then arrived, determined that Marilyn was dead, examined his brother's injuries, and removed him to the nearby clinic operated by the Sheppard family.[3] When the Coroner, the Cleveland police and other officials arrived, the house and surrounding area were thoroughly searched, the rooms of the house were photographed, and many per-

---

[2] The several witnesses to whom Sheppard narrated his experiences differ in their description of various details. Sheppard claimed the vagueness of his perception was caused by his sudden awakening, the dimness of the light, and his loss of consciousness.

[3] Sheppard was suffering from severe pain in his neck, a swollen eye, and shock.

sons, including the Houks and the Aherns, were interrogated. The Sheppard home and premises were taken into "protective custody" and remained so until after the trial.[4]

From the outset officials focused suspicion on Sheppard. After a search of the house and premises on the morning of the tragedy, Dr. Gerber, the Coroner, is reported—and it is undenied—to have told his men, "Well, it is evident the doctor did this, so let's go get the confession out of him." He proceeded to interrogate and examine Sheppard while the latter was under sedation in his hospital room. On the same occasion, the Coroner was given the clothes Sheppard wore at the time of the tragedy together with the personal items in them. Later that afternoon Chief Eaton and two Cleveland police officers interrogated Sheppard at some length, confronting him with evidence and demanding explanations. Asked by Officer Shotke to take a lie detector test, Sheppard said he would if it were reliable. Shotke replied that it was "infallible" and "you might as well tell us all about it now." At the end of the interrogation Shotke told Sheppard: "I think you killed your wife." Still later in the same afternoon a physician sent by the Coroner was permitted to make a detailed examination of Sheppard. Until the Coroner's inquest on July 22, at which time he was subpoenaed, Sheppard made himself available for frequent and extended questioning without the presence of an attorney.

On July 7, the day of Marilyn Sheppard's funeral, a newspaper story appeared in which Assistant County Attorney Mahon—later the chief prosecutor of Sheppard—sharply criticized the refusal of the Sheppard family to permit his immediate questioning. From there on headline stories repeatedly stressed Sheppard's lack of cooperation with the police and other officials. Under the headline "Testify Now In Death, Bay Doctor Is Ordered," one story described a visit by Coroner Gerber and four police officers to the hospital on July 8. When Sheppard insisted that his lawyer be present, the Coroner wrote out a subpoena and served it on him. Sheppard then agreed to submit to questioning without counsel and the subpoena was torn up. The officers questioned him for several hours. On July 9, Sheppard, at the

---

[4] But newspaper photographers and reporters were permitted access to Sheppard's home from time to time and took pictures throughout the premises.

request of the Coroner, re-enacted the tragedy at his home before the Coroner, police officers, and a group of newsmen, who apparently were invited by the Coroner. The home was locked so that Sheppard was obliged to wait outside until the Coroner arrived. Sheppard's performance was reported in detail by the news media along with photographs. The newspapers also played up Sheppard's refusal to take a lie detector test and "the protective ring" thrown up by his family. Front-page newspaper headlines announced on the same day that "Doctor Balks At Lie Test; Retells Story." A column opposite that story contained an "exclusive" interview with Sheppard headlined: " 'Loved My Wife, She Loved Me,' Sheppard Tells News Reporter." The next day, another headline story disclosed that Sheppard had "again late yesterday refused to take a lie detector test" and quoted an Assistant County Attorney as saying that "at the end of a nine-hour questioning of Dr. Sheppard, I felt he was now ruling [a test] out completely." But subsequent newspaper articles reported that the Coroner was still pushing Sheppard for a lie detector test. More stories appeared when Sheppard would not allow authorities to inject him with "truth serum." [5]

On the 20th, the "editorial artillery" opened fire with a front-page charge that somebody is "getting away with murder." The editorial attributed the ineptness of the investigation to "friendships, relationships, hired lawyers, a husband who ought to have been subjected instantly to the same third-degree to which any other person under similar circumstances is subjected . . . ." The following day, July 21, another page-one editorial was headed: "Why No Inquest? Do It Now, Dr. Gerber." The Coroner called an inquest the same day and subpoenaed Sheppard. It was staged the next day in a School gymnasium; the Coroner presided with the County Prosecutor as his advisor and two detectives as bailiffs. In the front of the room was a long table occupied by reporters, television and radio personnel, and broadcasting equipment. The hearing was broadcast with live microphones placed at the Coroner's seat and the witness stand. A swarm

---

[5] At the same time, the newspapers reported that other possible suspects had been "cleared" by lie detector tests. One of these persons was quoted as saying that he could not understand why an innocent man would refuse to take such a test.

of reporters and photographers attended. Sheppard was brought into the room by police who searched him in full view of several hundred spectators. Sheppard's counsel were present during the three-day inquest but were not permitted to participate. When Sheppard's chief counsel attempted to place some documents in the record, he was forcibly ejected from the room by the Coroner, who received cheers, hugs, and kisses from ladies in the audience. Sheppard was questioned for five and one-half hours about his actions on the night of the murder, his married life, and a love affair with Susan Hayes.[6] At the end of the hearing the Coroner announced that he "could" order Sheppard held for the grand jury, but did not do so.

Throughout this period the newspapers emphasized evidence that tended to incriminate Sheppard and pointed out discrepancies in his statements to authorities. At the same time, Sheppard made many public statements to the press and wrote feature articles asserting his innocence.[7] During the inquest on July 26, a headline in large type stated: "Kerr [Captain of the Cleveland Police] Urges Sheppard's Arrest." In the story, Detective McArthur "disclosed that scientific tests at the Sheppard home have definitely established that the killer washed off a trail of blood from the murder bedroom to the downstairs section," a circumstance casting doubt on Sheppard's accounts of the murder. No such evidence was produced at trial. The newspapers also delved into Sheppard's personal life. Articles stressed his extra-marital love affairs as a motive for the crime. The newspapers portrayed Sheppard as a Lothario, fully explored his relationship with Susan Hayes, and named a number of other women who were allegedly involved with him. The testimony at trial never showed that Sheppard had any illicit relationships besides the one with Susan Hayes.

On July 28, an editorial entitled "Why Don't Police Quiz Top Suspect" demanded that Sheppard be taken to police headquarters. It described him in the following language: "Now proved under oath to be a liar, still free to go about his business, shielded by his family, protect-

---

[6] The newspapers had heavily emphasized Sheppard's illicit affair with Susan Hayes, and the fact that he had initially lied about it.

[7] A number of articles calculated to evoke sympathy for Sheppard were printed, such as the letters Sheppard wrote to his son while in jail. These stories often appeared together with news coverage which was unfavorable to him.

ed by a smart lawyer who has made monkeys of the police and authorities, carrying a gun part of the time, left free to do whatever he pleases . . . ." A front-page editorial on July 30 asked: "Why Isn't Sam Sheppard in Jail?" It was later titled "Quit Stalling—Bring Him In." After calling Sheppard "the most unusual murder suspect ever seen around these parts" the article said that "[e]xcept for some superficial questioning during Coroner Sam Gerber's inquest he has been scot-free of any official grilling . . . ." It asserted that he was "surrounded by an iron curtain of protection [and] concealment."

That night at 10 o'clock Sheppard was arrested at his father's home on a charge of murder. He was taken to the Bay Village City Hall where hundreds of people, newscasters, photographers and reporters were awaiting his arrival. He was immediately arraigned—having been denied a temporary delay to secure the presence of counsel—and bound over to the grand jury.

The publicity then grew in intensity until his indictment on August 17. Typical of the coverage during this period is a front-page interview entitled: "DR. SAM: 'I Wish There Was Something I Could Get Off My Chest—but There Isn't.'" Unfavorable publicity included items such as a cartoon of the body of a sphinx with Sheppard's head and the legend below: " 'I Will do Everything In My Power to Help Solve This Terrible Murder.'—Dr. Sam Sheppard." Headlines announced, *inter alia,* that: "Doctor Evidence is Ready for Jury," "Corrigan Tactics Stall Quizzing," "Sheppard 'Gay Set' Is Revealed By Houk," "Blood Is Found In Garage," "New Murder Evidence Is Found, Police Claim," "Dr. Sam Faces Quiz At Jail On Marilyn's Fear Of Him." On August 18, an article appeared under the headline "Dr. Sam Writes His Own Story." And reproduced across the entire front page was a portion of the typed statement signed by Sheppard: "I am not guilty of the murder of my wife, Marilyn. How could I, who have been trained to help people and devote my life to saving life, commit such a terrible and revolting crime?" We do not detail the coverage further. There are five volumes filled with similar clippings from each of the three Cleveland newspapers.covering the period from the murder until Sheppard's conviction in December 1954. The record includes no excerpts from newscasts on radio and television but since space was reserved in the courtroom for these media we assume that their coverage was equally large.

II

With this background the case came on for trial two weeks before the November general election at which the chief prosecutor was a candidate for municipal judge and the presiding judge, Judge Blythin, was a candidate to succeed himself. Twenty-five days before the case was set, a list of 75 veniremen were called as prospective jurors. This list, including the addresses of each venireman, was published in all three Cleveland newspapers. As a consequence, anonymous letters and telephone calls, as well as calls from friends, regarding the impending prosecution were received by all of the prospective jurors. The selection of the jury began on October 18, 1954.

The courtroom in which the trial was held measured 26 by 48 feet. A long temporary table was set up inside the bar, in back of the single counsel table. It ran the width of the courtroom, parallel to the bar railing, with one end less than three feet from the jury box. Approximately 20 representatives of newspapers and wire services were assigned seats at this table by the court. Behind the bar railing there were four rows of benches. These seats were likewise assigned by the court for the entire trial. The first row was occupied by representatives of television and radio stations, and the second and third rows by reporters from out-of-town newspapers and magazines. One side of the last row, which accommodated 14 people, was assigned to Sheppard's family and the other to Marilyn's. The public was permitted to fill vacancies in this row on special passes only. Representatives of the news media also used all the rooms on the courtroom floor, including the room where cases were ordinarily called and assigned for trial. Private telephone lines and telegraphic equipment were installed in these rooms so that reports from the trial could be speeded to the papers. Station WSRS was permitted to set up broadcasting facilities on the third floor of the courthouse next door to the jury room, where the jury rested during recesses in the trial and deliberated. Newscasts were made from this room throughout the trial, and while the jury reached its verdict.

On the sidewalk and steps in front of the courthouse, television and newsreel cameras were occasionally used to take motion pictures of the participants in the trial, including the jury and the judge. Indeed, one television broadcast carried a staged interview of the judge as he entered the courthouse. In the corridors outside the courtroom there was a host of photographers and television personnel with flash cameras, portable lights and motion picture cameras. This group photographed the prospective jurors during selection of the jury. After the trial opened, the witnesses, counsel, and jurors were photographed and televised whenever they entered or left the courtroom. Sheppard was brought to the courtroom about 10 minutes before each session began; he was surrounded by reporters and extensively photographed for the newspapers and television. A rule of court prohibited picture-taking in the courtroom during the actual session of the court, but no restraints were put on photographers during recesses, which were taken once each morning and afternoon, with a longer period for lunch.

All of these arrangements with the news media and their massive coverage of the trial continued during the entire nine weeks of the trial. The courtroom remained crowded to capacity with representatives of news media. Their movement in and out of the courtroom often caused so much confusion that, despite the loud speaker system installed in the courtroom, it was difficult for the witnesses and counsel to be heard. Furthermore, the reporters clustered within the bar of the small courtroom made confidential talk among Sheppard and his counsel almost impossible during the proceedings. They frequently had to leave the courtroom to obtain privacy. And many times when counsel wished to raise a point with the judge out of the hearing of the jury it was necessary to move to the judge's chambers. Even then, news media representatives so packed the judge's anteroom that counsel could hardly return from the chambers to the courtroom. The reporters vied with each other to find out what counsel and the judge had discussed, and often these matters later appeared in newspapers accessible to the jury.

The daily record of the proceedings was made available to the newspapers and the testimony of each witness was printed *verbatim* in the local editions, along with objections of counsel, and rulings by the judge. Pictures of Sheppard, the judge, counsel, pertinent witnesses, and the jury often accompanied the daily newspaper and television accounts. At times the newspapers published photographs of exhibits introduced at the trial, and the rooms of Sheppard's house were featured along with relevant testimony.

The jurors themselves were constantly exposed to the news media. Every juror, except one, testified at *voir dire* to reading about the case in the Cleveland papers or to having heard broadcasts about it. Seven of the 12 jurors who rendered the verdict had one or more Cleveland papers delivered in their home; the remaining jurors were not interrogated on the point. Nor were there questions as to radios or television sets in the jurors' homes, but we must assume that most of them owned such conveniences. As the selection of the jury progressed, individual pictures of prospective members appeared daily. During the trial, pictures of the jury appeared over 40 times in the Cleveland papers alone. The court permitted photographers to take pictures of the jury in the box, and individual pictures of the members in the jury room. One newspaper ran pictures of the jurors at the Sheppard home when they went there to view the scene of the murder. Another paper featured the home life of an alternate juror. The day before the verdict was rendered—while the jurors were at lunch and sequestered by two bailiffs—the jury was separated into two groups to pose for photographs which appeared in the newspapers.

III

We now reach the conduct of the trial. While the intense publicity continued unabated, it is sufficient to relate only the more flagrant episodes:

1. On October 9, 1954, nine days before the case went to trial, an editorial in one of the newspapers criticized defense counsel's random poll of people on the streets as to their opinion of Sheppard's guilt or innocence in an effort to use the resulting statistics to show the necessity for change of venue. The article said the survey "smacks of mass jury tampering," called on defense counsel to drop it, and stated that the bar association should do something about it. It characterized the poll as "non-judicial, non-legal, and nonsense." The article was called to the attention of the court but no action was taken.

2. On the second day of *voir dire* examination a debate was staged and broadcast live over WHK radio. The participants, newspaper reporters, accused Sheppard's counsel of throwing roadblocks in the way of the prosecution and asserted that Sheppard conceded his guilt by hiring a prominent criminal lawyer. Sheppard's counsel objected to this broadcast and requested a continuance, but the judge denied the motion. When counsel asked the court to give some protection from such events, the judge replied that "WHK doesn't have much coverage," and that "[a]fter all, we are not trying this case by radio or in newspapers or any other means. We confine ourselves seriously to it in this courtroom and do the very best we can."

3. While the jury was being selected, a two-inch headline asked: "But Who Will Speak for Marilyn?" The front-page story spoke of the "perfect face" of the accused. "Study that face as long as you want. Never will you get from it a hint of what might be the answer . . . ." The two brothers of the accused were described as "Prosperous, poised. His two sisters-in-law. Smart, chic, well-groomed. His elderly father. Courtly, reserved. A perfect type for the patriarch of a staunch clan." The author then noted Marilyn Sheppard was "still off stage," and that she was an only child whose mother died when she was very young and whose father had no interest in the case. But the author— through quotes from Detective Chief James McArthur—assured readers that the prosecution's exhibits would speak for Marilyn. "Her story," McArthur stated, "will come into this courtroom through our witnesses." The article ends:

"Then you realize how what and who is missing from the perfect setting will be supplied.

"How in the Big Case justice will be done.

"Justice to Sam Sheppard.

"And to Marilyn Sheppard."

4. As has been mentioned, the jury viewed the scene of the murder on the first day of the trial. Hundreds of reporters, cameramen and onlookers were there, and one representative of the news media was permitted to accompany the jury while it inspected the Sheppard home. The time of the jury's visit was revealed so far in advance that one of

the newspapers was able to rent a helicopter and fly over the house taking pictures of the jurors on their tour.

5. On November 19, a Cleveland police officer gave testimony that tended to contradict details in the written statement Sheppard made to the Cleveland police. Two days later, in a broadcast heard over Station WHK in Cleveland, Robert Considine likened Sheppard to a perjurer and compared the episode to Alger Hiss' confrontation with Whittaker Chambers. Though defense counsel asked the judge to question the jury to ascertain how many heard the broadcast, the court refused to do so. The judge also overruled the motion for continuance based on the same ground, saying: "Well, I don't know, we can't stop people, in any event, listening to it. It is a matter of free speech, and the court can't control everybody. . . . We are not going to harass the jury every morning. . . . It is getting to the point where if we do it every morning, we are suspecting the jury. I have confidence in this jury . . . ."

6. On November 24, a story appeared under an eight-column headline: "Sam Called A 'Jekyll-Hyde' By Marilyn, Cousin To Testify." It related that Marilyn had recently told friends that Sheppard was a "Dr. Jekyll and Mr. Hyde" character. No such testimony was ever produced at the trial. The story went on to announce: "The prosecution has a 'bombshell witness' on tap who will testify to Dr. Sam's display of fiery temper—countering the defense claim that the defendant is a gentle physician with an even disposition." Defense counsel made motions for change of venue, continuance and mistrial, but they were denied. No action was taken by the court.

7. When the trial was in its seventh week, Walter Winchell broadcasted over WXEL television and WJW radio that Carole Beasley, who was under arrest in New York City for robbery, had stated that, as Sheppard's mistress, she had borne him a child. The defense asked that the jury be queried on the broadcast. Two jurors admitted in open court that they had heard it. The judge asked each: "Would that have any effect upon your judgment?" Both replied, "No." This was accepted by the judge as sufficient; he merely asked the jury to "pay no attention whatever to that type of scavenging. . . . Let's confine ourselves to this courtroom, if you please." In answer to the motion for mistrial, the judge said:

"Well, even, so, Mr. Corrigan, how are you ever going to prevent those things, in any event? I don't justify them at all. I think it is outrageous, but in a sense, it is outrageous even if there were no trial here. The trial has nothing to do with it in the Court's mind, as far as its outrage is concerned, but—"

"Mr. CORRIGAN: I don't know what effect it had on the mind of any of these jurors, and I can't find out unless inquiry is made.

"The COURT: How would you ever, in any jury, avoid that kind of a thing?"

8. On December 9, while Sheppard was on the witness stand he testified that he had been mistreated by Cleveland detectives after his arrest. Although he was not at the trial, Captain Kerr of the Homicide Bureau issued a press statement denying Sheppard's allegations which appeared under the headline: " 'Bare-faced Liar,' Kerr Says of Sam." Captain Kerr never appeared as a witness at the trial.

9. After the case was submitted to the jury, it was sequestered for its deliberations, which took five days and four nights. After the verdict, defense counsel ascertained that the jurors had been allowed to make telephone calls to their homes every day while they were sequestered at the hotel. Although the telephones had been removed from the jurors' rooms, the jurors were permitted to use the phones in the bailiffs' rooms. The calls were placed by the jurors themselves; no record was kept of the jurors who made calls, the telephone numbers or the parties called. The bailiffs sat in the room where they could hear only the jurors' end of the conversation. The court had not instructed the bailiffs to prevent such calls. By a subsequent motion, defense counsel urged that this ground alone warranted a new trial, but the motion was overruled and no evidence was taken on the question.

IV

The principle that justice cannot survive behind walls of silence has long been reflected in the "Anglo-American distrust for secret trials." *In re Oliver,* 333 U. S. 257, 268 (1948). A responsible press has always been regarded as the handmaiden of effective judicial administration, especially in the criminal field. Its function in this regard is documented by an impressive record of service over several centuries. The press does not simply publish information about trials but guards against the miscarriage of justice by subjecting the police, prosecutors, and judicial processes to extensive public scrutiny and criticism. This Court has, therefore, been unwilling to place any direct limitations on the freedom traditionally exercised by the news media for "[w]hat transpires in the court room is public property." *Craig* v. *Harney,* 331 U. S. 367, 374 (1947). The "unqualified prohibitions laid down by the framers were intended to give to liberty of the press . . . the broadest scope that could be countenanced in an orderly society." *Bridges* v. *California,* 314 U. S. 252, 265 (1941). And where there was "no threat or menace to the integrity of the trial," *Craig* v. *Harney, supra,* at 377, we have consistently required that the press have a free hand, even though we sometimes deplored its sensationalism.

But the Court has also pointed out that "[l]egal trials are not like elections, to be won through the use of the meeting-hall, the radio, and the newspaper." *Bridges* v. *California, supra,* at 271. And the Court has insisted that no one be punished for a crime without "a charge fairly made and fairly tried in a public tribunal free of prejudice, passion, excitement, and tyranical power." *Chambers* v. *Florida,* 309 U. S. 227, 236–237 (1940). "Freedom of discussion should be given the widest range compatible with the essential requirement of the fair and orderly administration of justice." *Pennekamp* v. *Florida,* 328 U. S. 331, 347 (1946). But it must not be allowed to divert the trial from the "very purpose of a court system . . . to adjudicate controversies, both criminal and civil, in the calmness and solemnity of the courtroom according to legal procedures." *Cox* v. *Louisiana,* 379 U. S. 559, 583 (1965) (BLACK, J., dissenting). Among these "legal procedures" is the requirement that the jury's verdict be based on evidence received in open court, not from outside sources. Thus, in *Marshall* v. *United States,* 360 U. S. 310 (1959), we set aside a federal conviction where the jurors were exposed "through news accounts" to information that was not admitted at trial. We held that the prejudice from such material "may indeed be greater" than when it is part of the prosecution's evidence "for it is then not tempered by protective procedures." At 313. At the same time, we did not consider dispositive the statement of each juror "that he would not be influenced by the news articles, that he could decide the case only on the evidence of record, and that he felt no prejudice against petitioner as a result of the articles." At 312. Likewise, in *Irvin* v. *Dowd,* 366 U. S. 717 (1961), even though each juror indicated that he could render an impartial verdict despite exposure to prejudicial newspaper articles, we set aside the conviction holding: "With his life at stake, it is not requiring too much that petitioner be tried in an atmosphere undisturbed by so huge a wave of public passion. . . ." At 728.

The undeviating rule of this Court was expressed by Mr. Justice Holmes over half a century ago in *Patterson* v. *Colorado,* 205 U. S. 454, 462 (1907): "The theory of our system is that the conclusions to be reached in a case will be induced only by evidence and argument in open court, and not by any outside influence, whether of private talk or public print." Moreover, "the burden of showing essential unfairness . . . as a demonstrable reality," *Adams* v. *United States ex rel. McCann,* 317 U. S. 269, 281 (1942), need not be undertaken when television has exposed the community "repeatedly and in depth to the spectacle of [the accused] personally confessing in detail to the crimes with which he was later to be charged." *Rideau* v. *Louisiana,* 373 U. S. 723, 726 (1963). In *Turner* v. *Louisiana,* 379 U. S. 466 (1965), two key witnesses were deputy sheriffs who doubled as jury shepherds during the trial. The deputies swore that they had not talked to the jurors about the case, but the Court nonetheless held that, "even if it could be assumed that the deputies never did discuss the case directly with any members of the jury, it would be blinking reality not to recognize the extreme prejudice inherent in this continual association . . . ." At 473.

Only last Term in *Estes* v. *Texas,* 381 U. S. 532 (1965), we set aside a conviction despite the absence of any showing of prejudice. We said there: "It is true that in most cases involving claims of due process deprivations we require a showing of identifiable prejudice to the accused. Nevertheless, at times a procedure employed by the State involves such a probability that prejudice will result that it is deemed inherently lacking in due process." At 542–543. And we cited with approval the language of MR. JUSTICE BLACK for the Court in *In re Murchison,* 349 U. S. 133, 136 (1955), that "our system of law has always endeavored to prevent even the probability of unfairness."

V

It is clear that the totality of circumstances in this case also warrant such an approach. Unlike Estes, Sheppard was not granted a change of venue to a locale away from where the publicity originated; nor was his jury sequestered. The Estes jury saw none of the television broadcasts from the courtroom. On the contrary, the Sheppard jurors were subjected to newspaper, radio and television coverage of the trial while not taking part in the proceedings. They were allowed to go their separate ways outside of the courtroom, without adequate directions not to read or listen to anything concerning the case. The judge's "admonitions" at the beginning of the trial are representative: "I would suggest to you and caution you that you do not read any newspapers during the progress of this trial, that you do not listen to radio comments nor watch or listen to television comments, insofar as this case is concerned. You will feel very much better as the trial proceeds . . . . I am sure that we shall all feel very much better if we do not indulge in any newspaper reading or listening to any comments whatever about the matter while the case is in progress. After it is all over, you can read it all to your heart's content . . . ." At intervals during the trial, the judge simply repeated his "suggestions" and "requests" that the jury not expose themselves to comment upon the case. Moreover, the jurors were thrust into the role of celebrities by the judge's failure to insulate them from reporters and photographers. See *Estes* v. *Texas, supra* at 545–546. The numerous pictures of the jurors, with their addresses, which appeared in the newspapers before and during the trial itself exposed them to expressions of opinion from both cranks and friends. The fact that anonymous letters had been received by prospective jurors should have made the judge aware that this publicity seriously threatened the jurors' privacy.

The press coverage of the Estes trial was not nearly as massive and persuasive as the attention given by the Cleveland newspapers and broadcasting stations to Sheppard's prosecution.[8] Sheppard stood indicted for the murder of his wife; the State was demanding the death penalty. For months the virulent publicity about Sheppard and the murder had made the case notorious. Charges and countercharges were aired in the news media besides those for which Sheppard was called to trial. In addition, only three months before trial, Sheppard was examined for more than five hours without counsel during a three-day inquest which ended in a public brawl. The inquest was televised live from a high school gymnasium seating hundreds of people. Furthermore, the trial began two weeks before a hotly contested election at which both Chief Prosecutor Mahon and Judge Blythin were candidates for judgeships.[9]

While we cannot say that Sheppard was denied due process by the judge's refusal to take precautions against the influence of pretrial publicity alone, the court's later rulings must be considered against the setting in which the trial was held. In light of this background, we believe that the arrangements made by the judge with the news media caused Sheppard to be deprived of that "judicial serenity and calm to which [he] was entitled." *Estes* v. *Texas, supra,* at 536. The fact is that bedlam reigned at the courthouse during the trial and newsmen took over practically the entire courtroom, hounding most of the participants in the trial, especially Sheppard. At a temporary table within a few feet of the jury box and counsel table sat some 20 reporters staring at Sheppard and taking notes. The erection of a press table for

[8] Many more reporters and photographers attended the Sheppard trial. And it attracted several nationally famous commentators as well.

[9] At the commencement of trial, defense counsel made motions for continuance and change of venue. The judge postponed ruling on these motions until he determined whether an impartial jury could be impaneled. *Voir dire* examination showed that with one exception all members selected for jury service had read something about the case in the newspapers. Since, however, all of the jurors stated that they would not be influenced by what they had read or seen, the judge overruled both of the motions. Without regard to whether the judge's actions in this respect reach dimensions that would justify issuance of the habeas writ, it should be noted that a short continuance would have alleviated any problem with regard to the judicial elections. The court in *Delaney* v. *United States,* 199 F. 2d 107, 115 (C. A. 1st Cir. 1952), recognized such a duty under similar circumstances, holding that "if assurance of a fair trial would necessitate that the trial of the case be postponed until after the election, then we think the law required no less than that."

reporters inside the bar is unprecedented. The bar of the court is reserved for counsel, providing them a safe place in which to keep papers and exhibits, and to confer privately with client and co-counsel. It is designed to protect the witness and the jury from any distractions, intrusions or influences, and to permit bench discussions of the judge's rulings away from the hearing of the public and the jury. Having assigned almost all of the available seats in the courtroom to the news media the judge lost his ability to supervise that environment. The movement of the reporters in and out of the courtroom caused frequent confusion and disruption of the trial. And the record reveals constant commotion within the bar. Moreover, the judge gave the throng of newsmen gathered in the corridors of the courthouse absolute free rein. Participants in the trial, including the jury, were forced to run a gauntlet of reporters and photographers each time they entered or left the courtroom. The total lack of consideration for the privacy of the jury was demonstrated by the assignment to a broadcasting station of space next to the jury room on the floor above the courtroom, as well as the fact that jurors were allowed to make telephone calls during their five-day deliberation.

VI

There can be no question about the nature of the publicity which surrounded Sheppard's trial. We agree, as did the Court of Appeals, with the findings in Judge Bell's opinion for the Ohio Supreme Court: "Murder and mystery, society, sex and suspense were combined in this case in such a manner as to intrigue and captivate the public fancy to a degree perhaps unparalleled in recent annals. Throughout the preindictment investigation, the subsequent legal skirmishes and the nine-week trial, circulation-conscious editors catered to the insatiable interest of the American public in the bizarre. . . . In this atmosphere of a 'Roman holiday' for the news media, Sam Sheppard stood trial for his life." 165 Ohio St., at 294. Indeed, every court that has considered this case, save the court that tried it, has deplored the manner in which the news media inflamed and prejudiced the public.[10]

---

[10] Typical comments on the trial by the press itself include:

"The question of Dr. Sheppard's guilt or innocence still is before the courts. Those who have examined the trial record carefully are divided as to the pro-

Much of the material printed or broadcast during the trial was never heard from the witness stand, such as the charges that Sheppard had purposely impeded the murder investigation and must be guilty since he had hired a prominent criminal lawyer; that Sheppard was a perjuror; that he had sexual relations with numerous women; that his slain wife had characterized him as a "Jekyll-Hyde"; that he was "a bare-faced liar" because of his testimony as to police treatment; and, finally, that a woman convict claimed Sheppard to be the father of her illegitimate child. As the trial progressed, the newspapers summarized and interpreted the evidence, devoting particular attention to the material that incriminated Sheppard, and often drew unwarranted inferences from testimony. At one point, a front-page picture of Mrs. Sheppard's blood-stained pillow was published after being "doctored" to show more clearly an alleged imprint of a surgical instrument.

Nor is there doubt that this deluge of publicity reached at least some of the jury. On the only occasion that the jury was queried, two jurors admitted in open court to hearing the highly inflammatory charge that a prison inmate claimed Sheppard as the father of her illegitimate child. Despite the extent and nature of the publicity to which the jury was exposed during the trial, the judge refused defense counsel's other requests that the jury be asked whether they had read or heard specific prejudicial comment about the case, including the incidents we have previously summarized. In these circumstances, we can assume that some of this material reached members of the jury. See *Commonwealth* v. *Crehan*, 345 Mass. 609, 188 N. E. 2d 923 (1963).

VII

The court's fundamental error is compounded by the holding that it lacked power to control the publicity about the trial. From the very

---

priety of the verdict. But almost everyone who watched the performance of the Cleveland press agrees that a fair hearing for the defendant, in that area, would be a modern miracle." Harrison, "The Press vs. the Courts," The Saturday Review (Oct. 15, 1955).

"At this distance, some 100 miles from Cleveland, it looks to us as though the Sheppard murder case was sensationalized to the point at which the press must ask itself if its freedom, carried to excess, doesn't interfere with the conduct of fair trials." Editorial, The Toledo Blade (Dec. 22, 1954).

inception of the proceedings the judge announced that neither he nor anyone else could restrict prejudicial news accounts. And he reiterated this view on numerous occasions. Since he viewed the news media as his target, the judge never considered other means that are often utilized to reduce the appearance of prejudicial material and to protect the jury from outside influence. We conclude that these procedures would have been sufficient to guarantee Sheppard a fair trial and so do not consider what sanctions might be available against a recalcitrant press nor the charges of bias now made against the state trial judge.[11]

The carnival atmosphere at trial could easily have been avoided since the courtroom and courthouse premises are subject to the control of the court. As we stressed in *Estes*, the presence of the press at judicial proceedings must be limited when it is apparent that the accused might otherwise be prejudged or disadvantaged.[12] Bearing in mind the massive pretrial publicity, the judge should have adopted stricter rules governing the use of the courtroom by newsmen, as Sheppard's counsel requested. The number of reporters in the courtroom itself could have been limited at the first sign that their presence would disrupt the trial. They certainly should not have been placed inside the bar. Furthermore, the judge should have more closely regulated the conduct of newsmen in the courtroom. For instance, the judge belatedly asked them not to handle and photograph trial exhibits laying on the counsel table during recesses.

Secondly, the court should have insulated the witnesses. All of the newspapers and radio stations apparently interviewed prospective witnesses at will, and in many instances disclosed their testimony. A typical example was the publication of numerous statements by Susan Hayes, before her appearance in court, regarding her love affair with Sheppard. Although the witnesses were barred from the courtroom

---

[11] In an unsworn statement, which the parties agreed would have the status of a deposition, made 10 years after Sheppard's conviction and six years after Judge Blythin's death, Dorothy Kilgallen asserted that Judge Blythin had told her: "It's an open and shut case . . . he is guilty as hell." It is thus urged that Sheppard be released on the ground that the judge's bias infected the entire trial. But we need not reach this argument, since the judge's failure to insulate the proceedings from prejudicial publicity and disruptive influences deprived Sheppard of the chance to receive a fair hearing.

[12] The judge's awareness of his power in this respect is manifest from his assignment of seats to the press.

during the trial the full verbatim testimony was available to them in the press. This completely nullified the judge's imposition of the rule. See *Estes* v. *Texas, supra,* at 547.

Thirdly, the court should have made some effort to control the release of leads, information, and gossip to the press by police officers, witnesses, and the counsel for both sides. Much of the information thus disclosed was inaccurate, leading to groundless rumors and confusion.[13] That the judge was aware of his responsibility in this respect may be seen from his warning to Steve Sheppard, the accused's brother, who had apparently made public statements in an attempt to discredit testimony for the prosecution. The judge made this statement in the presence of the jury:

"Now, the Court wants to say a word. That he was told—he has not read anything about it at all—but he was informed that Dr. Steve Sheppard, who has been granted the privilege of remaining in the courtroom during the trial, has been trying the case in the newspapers and making rather uncomplimentary comments about the testimony of the witnesses for the State.

"Let it be now understood that if Dr. Steve Sheppard wishes to use the newspapers to try his case while we are trying it here, he will be barred from remaining in the courtroom during the progress of the trial if he is to be a witness in the case.

"The Court appreciates he cannot deny Steve Sheppard the right of free speech, but he can deny him the . . . privilege of being in the courtroom, if he wants to avail himself of that method during the progress of the trial."

Defense counsel immediately brought to the court's attention the tremendous amount of publicity in the Cleveland press that "misrepre-

---

[13] The problem here was further complicated by the independent action of the newspapers in reporting "evidence" and gossip which they uncovered. The press not only inferred that Sheppard was guilty because he "stalled" the investigation, hid behind his family, and hired a prominent criminal lawyer, but denounced as "mass jury tampering" his efforts to gather evidence of community prejudice caused by such publications. Sheppard's counterattacks added some fuel but, in these circumstances, cannot preclude him from asserting his right to a fair trial. Putting to one side news stories attributed to police officials, prospective witnesses, the Sheppards, and the lawyers, it is possible that the other publicity "would itself have had a prejudicial effect." See Report of the President's Commission on the Assassination of President Kennedy, at 239.

sented entirely the testimony" in the case. Under such circumstances, the judge should have at least warned the newspapers to check the accuracy of their accounts. And it is obvious that the judge should have further sought to alleviate this problem by imposing control over the statements made to the news media by counsel, witnesses, and especially the Coroner and police officers. The prosecution repeatedly made evidence available to the news media which was never offered in the trial. Much of the "evidence" disseminated in this fashion was clearly inadmissible. The exclusion of such evidence in court is rendered meaningless when a news media makes it available to the public. For example, the publicity about Sheppard's refusal to take a lie detector test came directly from police officers and the Coroner.[14] The story that Sheppard had been called a "Jekyll-Hyde" personality by his wife was attributed to a prosecution witness. No such testimony was given. The further report that there was "a 'bombshell witness' on tap" who would testify as to Sheppard's "fiery temper" could only have emanated from the prosecution. Moreover, the newspapers described in detail clues that had been found by the police, but not put into the record.[15]

The fact that many of the prejudicial news items can be traced to the prosecution, as well as the defense, aggravates the judge's failure to take any action. See *Stroble* v. *California,* 343 U. S. 181, 201 (1952) (Frankfurter, J., dissenting). Effective control of these sources —concededly within the court's power—might well have prevented the divulgence of inaccurate information, rumors, and accusations that made up much of the inflammatory publicity, at least after Sheppard's indictment.

More specifically, the trial court might well have proscribed extra-judicial statements by any lawyer, party, witness, or court official

---

[14] When two officers testified at trial that Sheppard refused to take a lie detector test, the judge declined to give a requested instruction that the results of such a test would be inadmissible in any event. He simply told the jury that no person has an obligation "to take any lie detector test."

[15] Such "premature disclosure and weighing of the evidence" may seriously jeopardize a defendant's right to an impartial jury. "[N]either the press nor the public had a right to be contemporaneously informed by the police or prosecuting authorities of the details of the evidence being accumulated against [Sheppard]." Report of the President's Commission, *supra,* at 239–240.

which divulged prejudicial matters, such as the refusal of Sheppard to submit to interrogation or take any lie detector tests; any statement made by Sheppard to officials; the identity of prospective witnesses or their probable testimony; any belief in guilt or innocence; or like statements concerning the merits of the case. See *State* v. *Van Duyne*, 43 N. J. 369, 389, 204 A. 2d 841, 852 (1964), in which the court interpreted Canon 20 of the American Bar Association's Canons of Professional Ethics to prohibit such statements. Being advised of the great public interest in the case, the mass coverage of the press, and the potential prejudicial impact of publicity, the court could also have requested the appropriate city and county officials to promulgate a regulation with respect to dissemination of information about the case by their employees.[16] In addition, reporters who wrote or broadcast prejudicial stories, could have been warned as to the impropriety of publishing material not introduced in the proceedings. The judge was put on notice of such events by defense counsel's complaint about the WHK broadcast on the second day of trial. See p. . . . [79], *supra.* In this manner, Sheppard's right to a trial free from outside interference would have been given added protection without corresponding curtailment of the news media. Had the judge, the other officers of the court, and the police placed the interest of justice first, the news media would have soon learned to be content with the task of reporting the case as it unfolded in the courtroom—not pieced together from extra-judicial statements.

From the cases coming here we note that unfair and prejudicial news comment on pending trials has become increasingly prevalent. Due process requires that the accused receive a trial by an impartial jury free from outside influences. Given the pervasiveness of modern communications and the difficulty of effacing prejudicial publicity from the minds of the jurors, the trial courts must take strong measures to ensure that the balance is never weighed against the accused. And appellate tribunals have the duty to make an independent evalua-

---

[16] The Department of Justice, the City of New York, and other governmental agencies have issued such regulations. *E. g.,* 28 CFR § 50.2 (1966). For general information on this topic see periodic publications (*e. g.,* Nos. 71, 124, and 158) by the Freedom of Information Center, School of Journalism, University of Missouri.

tion of the circumstances. Of course, there is nothing that proscribes the press from reporting events that transpire in the courtroom. But where there is a reasonable likelihood that prejudicial news prior to trial will prevent a fair trial, the judge should continue the case until the threat abates, or transfer it to another county not so permeated with publicity. In addition, sequestration of the jury was something the judge should have raised *sua sponte* with counsel. If publicity during the proceedings threatens the fairness of the trial, a new trial should be ordered. But we must remember that reversals are but palliatives; the cure lies in those remedial measures that will prevent the prejudice at its inception. The courts must take such steps by rule and regulation that will protect their processes from prejudicial outside interferences. Neither prosecutors, counsel for defense, the accused, witnesses, court staff nor enforcement officers coming under the jurisdiction of the court should be permitted to frustrate its function. Collaboration between counsel and the press as to information affecting the fairness of a criminal trial is not only subject to regulation, but is highly censurable and worthy of disciplinary measures.

Since the state trial judge did not fulfill his duty to protect Sheppard from the inherently prejudicial publicity which saturated the community and to control disruptive influences in the courtroom, we must reverse the denial of the habeas petition. The case is remanded to the District Court with instructions to issue the writ and order that Sheppard be released from custody unless the State puts him to its charges again within a reasonable time.

It is so ordered.

Mr. Justice Black dissents.

TABLE OF CASES CITED

INDEX